Costume in Greek Classic Drama

Costume in
Greek Classic Drama

IRIS BROOKE

GREENWOOD PRESS, PUBLISHERS
WESTPORT, CONNECTICUT

PA
3203
B75
1973

Library of Congress Cataloging in Publication Data

Brooke, Iris.
    Costume in Greek classic drama.

    Reprint of the ed. published by Methuen, London.
    1. Theater--Greece.   2. Costume--History--Ancient.
I. Title.
[PA3203.B75 1973]   792'.026'0938   73-3010
ISBN 0-8371-6828-7

First published in 1962 by Methuen & Co. Ltd., London

Reprinted by Greenwood Press, Inc.

First Greenwood reprinting 1973
Second Greenwood reprinting 1977

Library of Congress Catalog Card Number 73-3010

ISBN 0-8371-6828-7

Printed in the United States of America

TO JANE KITTO

Contents

Illustrations

Acknowledgements

Without the very valuable assistance of many of my friends and colleagues in the Department of Classics, Bristol University, this book would probably never have been achieved. For with such help I have managed to obtain fresh translations from the passages which bear upon costume details so that I am able to emphasize particular interesting points. Chief amongst such friends is Professor Kitto who read my first rough copy and added many apt and stimulating suggestions and comments. My investigations have been aided greatly by the award of a Research Grant from the University that enabled me to go to Greece and make drawings and actually handle much of the smaller statuary as well as sense the atmosphere of the great theatres that still retain much of their original significance.

The Staff of the British School at Athens smoothed my paths in many directions; I am also indebted to the Museo Nazionale at Naples who gave me every possible assistance.

For translations and double checkings of difficult passages and puzzling drawings I am chiefly beholden to James Tester, Professor John Cook, David Campbell, Michael Wotton and a young friend and neighbour John Hawks, who has since won a Classics scholarship to Cambridge.

The books that I have found most useful are those by Sir Arthur Pickard-Cambridge, *The Theatre of Dionysus at Athens* and *Dramatic Festivals at Athens*, Professor W. Beare's *The Roman Stage*, Professor T. B. L. Webster's *Greek Theatre Production*, Martin Robertson's Skira book on *Greek Paintings* and of course the works of Professor H. D. F. Kitto. Each of these specialists has thrown a different light on a fascinating and elusive subject.

Of other friends Jane Kitto, who nobly retyped the whole book for me under some considerable pressure for time, deserves more than an acknowledgement – so I have dedicated the book to her as a small token of my very great appreciation.

Fig. 1A. The Rehearsal, Pompeii, 1st cent. A.D.

Fig. 1B. Hercules, flute player, satyr, from Pronomos Vase, 5th cent. B.C.

Introduction

The importance of costume in the theatre cannot be rated too highly, for it is not only an outward and immediately visible medium of expression for the actor himself but it is significant of the dramatic values which he is supposed to portray. Its character, whatever it may be, can be expressed by the subtle use of appropriate colours, textures and designs; by the manner in which it is worn, by signs and tokens of identity. This fact, if we are to believe the evidence of pictorial forms of the fifth century B.C., was one of considerable interest to all Greek artists. Elimination of unnecessary detail and exaggeration of significant form was the keynote of artistic achievement.

In the following pages I have very frequently referred to the works of Homer (such references throughout are taken from the translation of Dr E. V. Rieu in Penguin Classics). My intention in so doing is to stress the source of poetic grandeur that inspired the dramatists' vision of costume. No detail of dress to Homer was insignificant, and whenever opportunity offered some glittering description emerges – often literally shot through with threads of gold. But to treat such references as factual evidence of fashions of one particular date is dangerous, for the works of Homer have been altered time and again by the copyists in succeeding ages. The costume descriptions as we read them now do not portray the clothes of archaic times but are much nearer to the clothes worn in the fifth century B.C. and certainly comparable with the illustrations of Homeric legend painted at this date. No one can insist that this is the correct attitude to accept regarding dramatic costume, but it is a possible attitude and one not unduly earthbound by archaeological research. It seems a very reasonable assumption that, in order to draw attention to some character and insist that he should not be overlooked, that character should be dressed in grander and more striking style than his companions. This is quite obviously a practice that has persisted from time immemorial and there is no good reason to suppose that the Greek dramatists were not as aware of this as any other civilized community. One does not normally go out of one's way to confuse an audience if there is a story to be told with clarity and meaning; it is only the modern trend towards a gimmick attraction that sets out to confuse in order to hold the supposedly jaded attention of a too critical audience. The very grandeur of Greek drama and the size of the vast theatres where the dramatic festivals originally took place, cried out for spectacle. The clothes of the fifth century were both simple and splendid and it could not have been difficult to find suitably dramatic attire based on the patterns of the day. In fact it is quite impossible to read any of the plays written by the ancient dramatists without realizing something of the spectacle that must have existed in their action, and the vast space that was provided for such action was obviously made use of to the full. The chariots of Agamemnon, the rolling out of the brilliant carpet, the funeral procession of Ajax, the procession at the climax of the *Eumenides*, and many other examples, are all vividly told and should be vividly enacted.

This book aims to give all available detail that might be of use to anyone interested in drama and in search of information, and also that might help him to obtain an impression of the vivid aspect of classical drama. Such details cover the period from the fifth century B.C., when the plays of Aeschylus, Sophocles, Euripides and Aristophanes were new, and compare them with the second century A.D., when Julius Pollux was writing of Hellenistic times and Imperial Rome, when costume had become a sort of formalized version of what the Romans imagined had been the Greek classic style. There is a difference which is obvious in contemporary works, and Pollux's insistence that Roman theatre costumes were in the Greek tradition is as inaccurate as the various classic revivals have been at different periods in our history. This I will endeavour to clarify later.

The subject is, to put it mildly, a confusing one and fraught with problems for the scholar. Definite information about the earliest Greek theatre costume is impossible, for so much time has elapsed since authentic records were made, and many authorities at a later date laid down laws and theories that cannot reasonably be sustained. What little we do know is taken from pictures that may quite possibly have been a stylized impression of the plays themselves; they may, on the other hand, have been the artist's ideal picturing of the myths from which all the dramatists originally took their characters and plots. The inclusion of masks in many groups may indicate nothing more than that this was a play; the painter may not have been trying to give a photographic likeness. We can, however, piece together such information as is available and see the fashionable or contemporary ideal which was introduced into sculpture and pictorial design; we can also pick out the many descriptive details and fragments of information given in the plays themselves. With careful consideration of these fragmentary indications an interesting fact emerges: that at the time when Greek drama was at its finest the costume also was at its most decorative and splendid. Attic fashions or conventions in characterization bear the imprint of genius. During a short half-century at least, the illustrative material that exists gives us a brilliant and tantalizing glimpse into the unbelievably dramatic vitality of this period.

The majority of our most valuable information about classic costume is to be found decorating the pottery of this date, much of which is preserved for our inspection in museums throughout the world. Despite the vast amount of material surviving, research in this instance is probably more confusing than in any other field, for we are immediately confronted with distortion and surface damage. Both these factors in themselves are distracting, but together they combine to make photographic reproduction so much poorer than the original that in many cases there is no possibility of distinguishing any of the figures. How much the natural distortion that arises from painting on a curved surface is increased by photographic reproduction varies considerably, but it is a real obstacle to anything approaching a clear picture. I have therefore been at pains to illustrate these pages from drawings that I have done from the actual vases, terra-cottas and small ornaments as well as the better-known statuary that is to be found in museums throughout Europe. Such ornaments were fashioned with delicacy and precision; their very realism makes an interesting comparison with the more conventional drawings of the potters. Golden fillets and wreaths have also been preserved as has a vast amount of jewellery and personal toilet trinkets. The majority of these elegant trifles can be dated without too much difficulty. The statuettes in bronze, silver or terra-cotta show the styles of hairdressing and the intricacies of fashionable draperies, and without these little figures we should be unaware of the three-dimensional effect, for no drawing or photograph can be entirely revealing. Our interest is to dress real people and that too was the problem in the classic theatre. The actors must move, sometimes with considerable violence, across a "place" where their movements were observed from every angle. There was no picture-frame stage at the theatre of Dionysus.

There are, and always have been, various schools of thought about the exact meaning of the term Classic Dramatic costume, and because we know from dozens of different sources that the traditional costume of comedy was by no means normal civil attire but was an exaggeration of all the less praiseworthy habits of an uninhibited society we may perhaps assume that the more ornate vases decorated with heroic figures do actually show theatrical costume. This may possibly have been true in some cases, but on the same vases one frequently finds nude figures representing the demi-gods, heroes and warriors. Obviously no actor appeared in the theatre with nothing but a hat and a pair of boots any more than people appeared on the streets without any covering – still less on the battlefield. Such illustrations are then proved fairly conclusively to be artist's licence. Nevertheless, these fifth-century decorations do give us really valuable information if we are seeking dramatic inspiration for costume. The same severe reticence in arrangement of drapery persists as in other illustrative material of the time, but these heroes and heroines are picked out in a grander style. Their patterns are certainly clear, distinctive patterns, that could be easily recognized by an audience seated, for instance, in the vast theatre of Epidaurus.

Such is one source of information, apart from wall paintings and mosaics of a later date, and such are its limitations. The other source is the plays themselves; the actual words (or translations of such words) from the hand of the playwright; given eyes and ears to see and hear we can gather together these fragile hints that can otherwise be ignored or disregarded so easily because the modern mind does not understand their true significance. Even here we are faced with a variety of hurdles because each of the copyists in ancient times may have made individual small alterations in the text, to fit some detail with which he was unfamiliar into his contemporary vocabulary. Also there still are many words which defy a clear-cut translation. One particular instance of this occurs in the *Suppliants* of Aeschylus. Seeking a clearer translation for the delightful passage describing the Danaids' clothing I came up against an apparently insuperable obstacle. The word (ἀμπύκωμα) which I have put in as *diadems* (see p. 95) has apparently two (or even three) distinct meanings. The Scholiast (on *Iliad* v. 358) says that this meant a gold band holding together the hair on horses' foreheads. The band which served the same purpose for women was sometimes also of gold. This particular word is in any case an emendation for the manuscript reading, which is retained in some editions and seems to mean literally "thick cloths" or could perhaps signify "deep folds", both of which give a reasonable sense, though there are numerous conjectures attempting to clarify the manuscript.

This is the sort of obstacle that does not appear to have a way around, and it is pretty useless to spend much time trying to remove it if it has caused trouble for so many years; we must do the best we can with the material available and face it with a little common sense. If the Danaids were intended to be obviously foreign visitors from a hotter country, it would seem unreasonable for them to be wearing thick clothes. The headdress, on the other hand, could be something unusual and remarkable, indicative of the fact that they were not only princesses wearing golden crowns but that they were not wearing the normal Sakkos that most Greek women at that particular time considered a very necessary ornament for their heads – "This is not the female dress of Argos nor yet of the land of Greece."

Problems of this sort occur not once but many times, so that nothing can be certain though something is suggested; perhaps this is better from a designer's point of view than too much indisputable evidence.

We cannot look for indisputable help, for no passage gives a full description of any one costume (though Aristophanes gives us a lot of information in *Lysistrata* and *Peace*). But certain crumbs of comfort can be gathered and these tell their tale, which plainly is that the original actors followed the patterns of their own age. Orestes, for instance, in Sophocles' *Electra*, must necessarily have long hair – as we know from the pictures of the time all young men had – for he is able to cut off a lock and leave it on the altar. Electra herself must wear her chiton girdled so that she can offer her girdle as a poor sacrifice to the gods. We are told that the fatal tunic in the *Women of Trachis*, sent by Deianeira to Heracles and impregnated with ghastly poison, was brilliant and gorgeous – her own work, woven in an intricate design or possibly embroidered with her own hands. All who saw it marvelled at its beauty. Deianeira also undid the golden buckle on her shoulder to lay bear her heart when she was about to stab herself. If her chiton had not been of the fashionable design there would have been no buckle to undo. These pins and buckles were a very necessary part of traditional costume, and we hear of a pin of another sort when Oedipus snatches those from Jocasta's shoulders to stab his eyes. Obviously these are the long pins which are still to be seen in any museum that has a collection of jewellery of Greek and Roman times. Of footwear also there are numerous details, from the buskins worn by Dionysus that appeared intensely feminine to Heracles in Aristophanes' *Frogs*, to the boots that Agamemnon takes off when he steps on to the purple carpet spread for him by Clytemnestra. Even little Persian slippers or sandals are mentioned in *Lysistrata*. These and many other apparently trifling details give pointers to the styles in which the actor played. By such details we can safely assume that the playwrights at least expected the actors to wear a costume identical in essentials to that worn at the time they were writing.

The dramatists were obviously well aware of the importance of visual presentation, and their personal differences of taste or feeling are made clear to us in one of Aristophanes' plays from which I shall quote. We are given to understand that Aeschylus set a standard in grandeur that confused and possibly irritated his followers. Euripides on the other hand introduced realism into his works in the form of rags and tatters, and other possibly relevant details that might have lowered the standard of presentation for a hyper-critical audience but perhaps had more appeal for the general public. However, Aristophanes makes a very interesting contribution to our knowledge of the manner in which these two dramatists saw their work presented. In the *Frogs*, Aeschylus and Euripides have an argument in which Euripides ridicules Aeschylus for being too highbrow and Aeschylus accuses Euripides of degrading the theatre by his earthiness.

> *Aeschylus:* Besides, it is right and proper for demigods to use grander words than we do: after all, they wear clothes much more magnificent than ours. I displayed them properly, but you maltreated them shamefully. *Euripides:* Why, what did I do? *Aeschylus:* First, you dressed your kings in rags, so that they might seem pitiable to the audience . . . (Aristophanes, *Frogs*, 1060 ff.).

Euripides, equally critical, declaims that Aeschylus

> was an imposter and a quack; I shall show you how he deceived the audience, taking them to be fools trained in Phrynichus' school. First he would set someone before them, some Achilles or Niobe, wrapping them up and not displaying their face, a sort of ornament to his tragedy, not even muttering a syllable. . . . Meanwhile the chorus might be laying it on with a string of lyrics, four in a row, perhaps: and *they* would still be silent. . . . This he did from sheer quackery, to

keep the audience in suspense, sitting waiting for Niobe to say something; and the play would be running on . . . And then when he'd drivelled on like this and the play was a good half done, he'd bull-roar a dozen words or so, proud words crested like cockerels, terrible bogey-words, that the spectators couldn't recognize . . . such as Scamanders and abysses and shields charged with brazen griffins, words to fall over and break your neck, so hard to understand" (ibid., 909 ff.).

Both dramatists claim that their inspiration comes from Homer, but with this essential difference. Aeschylus claims that "The poet should hide what is vile and not produce or represent it on the stage . . . we must only display what is good." Therefore the splendour of his costumes must be of primary importance. Euripides boasts that "I introduced into my plays our ordinary domestic affairs, in which all of us are concerned: on the basis of these I could be criticized, since all the audience knew about them and could criticize my art" (ibid., 959 ff.). From these fragmentary excerpts various essential differences in the style of production emerge. In all probability these were as marked as the differences between the designs used by Charles Kean and those of Gordon Craig.

As the tradition of theatre production was set in the fifth century B.C., the habits of that age are of particular interest to us, for tradition remained one of the most important governing factors throughout the period of classic drama. The works of the early dramatists were reproduced again and again in the ensuing centuries and, according to Pollux, the costumes remained unchanged. The statement cannot, however, be accepted in its entirety, for there are most definitely changes in styles during the seven hundred years that we are considering, and these changes are obvious to us even in the few remaining pictured examples of theatre costume. Let us take for instance two of the richest illustrations available to us, both in Naples Museum: the Pronomos vase with its famous satyr chorus and richly decorated costumes of the main characters, which is dated by experts at the end of the fifth century, and the mosaic of the "Rehearsal" from the ruins of Pompeii, designed some five hundred years later (see p. x). There are admittedly certain similarities between these, but the dissimilarities are more obvious. The most striking differences are, first, the high waistline of the flute player in the Pompeii mosaic (which gives the impression that the gown has a separate dark yoke), and the apparently normal waistline in the earlier example which indicates the flowing long-sleeved gown of highly decorated design which we must associate with the term "dramatic costume". Next, the two figures standing to the left of the mosaic and generally accepted as representing satyrs do not conform to the original satyr costume except for the short fur trunks. They have no tails, no phalloi, and at least one of them appears to be wearing a sort of vest. On top of the head of the other is something that resembles a flat, bird-like mask with two small feathers above it. This is not in any way similar to the original satyr masks which appear, not once but many times, in the drawings of the fifth century. It is, of course, possible that these figures were not intended to represent satyrs, but some other sort of animal chorus, and that the mask worn in the manner of the Corinthian helmet is, in fact, a much lighter affair than the full masks shown in the centre of the picture and obviously meant to be worn by the leading characters. It could, in fact, be a simplified chorus mask – simplified during the centuries so as to be more easily handled, and pushed up like a pair of spectacles when not in use. The other masks shown here are more grotesque than those drawn, with singular beauty, on the Greek vase. The exaggerated facial contortions of the Roman mask are in every instance more like a caricature from Hogarth or Bosch. However, the point is made, I hope, that the costumes did not remain identical but were quite naturally influenced by contemporary fashions and designers' tricks. The Romans were translating traditional form into their own idiom and this is permissible in any age.

I have endeavoured to illustrate the sort of costumes that might have been worn – and I have purposely eliminated anything of a complicated design that would have little or no theatrical appeal.

Certain obvious facts present themselves from a study of ancient drawings that should be accepted as a guide to designers. One of these is the importance of identification; insignia and peculiarities of god-like or foreign personalities. To the gods I have devoted a short chapter because they do make their appearance quite frequently. The foreigners are more difficult to determine because the classic artists so frequently assumed that all foreigners wore the same sort of costume. This attitude surely sprang from a lack of information rather than a true illustration, but nevertheless we find that characters such as Medea are nearly always pictured wearing " Asiatic" headdress.

The whole culture of the Greek world was simplified because of its comparative isolation. It is just this simplification that gives us a superb unhindered structure on which to build our designs for costume in classic drama.

CHAPTER I

Textiles and civil attire

A sort of paradox in designing costume for the theatre is: the greater the restrictions of the scheme imposed on the designer the greater the possibilities of significance in the design. It is, however, more than a mere paradox. For if a producer were to say to his designer, "I want this play dressed all in green", the problem for the designer would, in fact, be reduced, the need for perfect design and careful colour values would be magnified, any line or shape now without significance would become a glaring error in design.

On the other hand, a producer who has no interest in the visual side of the play and leaves his designer unguided is asking for trouble. In such a case it is far more difficult for the designer to help the actors in their parts because he is unaware of any overall scheme, conscious or unconscious. And if a scheme is not expressed in so many words beforehand, it cannot be discovered until the play is ready to go on the stage – and by then it is obviously too late to design costumes.

Let us for a moment suppose that we are designing for the gentleman with the green complex, and he is producing a classic play; where do we go for our necessary ideas? Preferably back to the time of the play's origin, because, by so doing, the shape as a whole and its original significance can be grasped. Whatever process of elimination or dressing up occurs afterwards is the business of the designer, but he has started off with several limitations which should help him to keep within certain bounds and produce simple and direct designs. If, however, his own interest in design is strictly governed by the desire to be different at all costs and to have nothing to do with the period about which the play is written, he is failing to make contact with anyone but himself, and instead of helping the actors or the producer he is creating an atmosphere alien to the play. Unless we are prepared to disregard large passages in any dramatist's work, we must consider for what reason he has introduced detailed descriptions of his own time. It is because he sees it that way. Shakespeare in modern

9

:ss has to be pretty heavily cut to make sense. So let us try to discover some-
.ing of what the dramatist saw in his lifetime and the inspiration that coloured
his works.

In the original productions of the fifth century B.C. the playwright was also
the producer and the designer, probably the chief actor too; so the result would
naturally have been all of a piece. His thoughts must have been directed towards the complete picture or series of pictures which probably crystallized and
took shape as the play was written. Now where did these ideas come from?
From the writings of Homer, we understand, for Homer was the bible of ancient
Greece. These were the golden stories of archaic times; their subject matter
the very roots from which sprang the flowers of Greek drama. It was Homer's
stirring descriptions of supernatural beings, fabulous monsters, terrifying
warriors in flashing armour, beautiful women in fine array and handsome
young heroes with the latest style in hairdressing that coloured the dramatist's
works. Their clothes and armour were as vividly described as their deeds of
valour or their voyages into unheard-of territories. Tragedy, violence and affec-
tion were all clothed in their appropriate costume.

The basis of all costume is the material from which it is made, for only with
certain materials can certain styles develop. For instance we cannot hope to give
a true impression of fifteenth-century costume if we use anything as transparent
and flimsy as nylon, because the very essence of fifteenth-century costume is its
dignified drapery, weight and swinging lines. We can, on the other hand,
adequately use a nylon silk for regency costume because here weight is neither
necessary nor desirable. The fabrics that were available to the ancient Greeks
were fabrics that they spun and wove themselves from their own supplies of
wool or linen. Homer gives specific details of the beauty and simplicity of these
fabrics. First he tells us that this elegant craft was carried out in the homes of
even the most nobly born – Pallas Athene herself is supposed to have woven her
own gown out of fine wool, and both Helen and Andromache, Hector's wife,
are pictured as being expert with the loom. The following passages give us
some interesting information. Iris bringing news to Helen,

> found Helen in her palace, at work on a great purple web of double width
> into which she was weaving some of the many battles between the horse-taming
> Trojans and the bronze-clad Achaeans in the war that had been forced upon them
> for her sake (*Iliad*, Bk. III).

Helen's gift to Telemachus,

> ... Helen, meanwhile, went to the chests which contained her embroidered dresses, the work of her own hands, and from them, great lady that she was, she lifted out the longest and most richly decorated robe which had lain underneath all the rest, and now glittered like a star ... (*Odyssey*, Bk. XV).

Andromache, when the news of Hector's death was brought to her,

> ... was at work in a corner of her lofty house on a purple web of double width which she was decorating with a floral pattern ...

Of particular interest at this stage is the fact that the materials might be wide, "of double width", and that they might be embroidered or have a pattern woven into them. Helen's gown that glittered like a star would probably have had gold or silver threads woven through it. We are clearly given to understand that weaving was an art like any other, and those with talent were in the advantageous position of being able to carry out their own designs. Because such fabrics were woven by hand and had such a deal of work and thought woven into them they were never cut, so that a whole garment was worked on the loom, its decoration woven into the texture of the material. After spinning and weaving had been perfected, it was so obviously more convenient to have a firmly woven edge or selvage down either side of the material. Therefore, ways and means of making such a length of material fit conveniently to the body were devised and developed. The Indian *sari* today is still an example of this and, though it bears no resemblance to the Greek chiton, it forms a perfect analogy. A certain amount of shaping can take place on a loom and no such possibilities seemed to escape the Greeks. Thus a shape in the form of a simple cross could form a tunic if there were an opening left in the weave at the centre of the fabric for the head to go through. Then it had only to be taken from the loom, folded over, the sides sewn together and the tunic was completed. Any sort of decoration on the hems could be done during the actual weaving. The dalmatic as we know it today is an unsewn version of this particular shape.

Two facts at this stage clearly govern the whole scheme of classic costume: first, the limits upon ingenuity set by a hand-loom – for example, weaving a scollop or chevron at one side of the material, or introducing any sort of complex design into the fabric – and second, the manner in which these lengths of material could be made up to give the best effect. The second of these problems is best resolved by consulting the pictures of the time, and then applying such knowledge as we have gained to the arrangement of the varying lengths and widths of the fabrics so that we can find something of the original effect. I shall deal with this side in the next chapter. At the moment we are still concerned with the materials themselves.

Let us consider the colours available and the forms of the designs woven into the fabrics; also the use of other textiles that are not mentioned by Homer but are to be found during the fifth century. Consider the references on the preceding page and see just what can be extracted from them about design and colour. First, Helen's weaving "... the many battles between the horse-taming Trojans and the bronze-clad Achaeans ... " This sentence does not in any way give us a picture of simplicity; it sounds remarkably complicated, more like the Bayeux tapestry than a woven design. Homer's meaning is clear – to give us an extravagant and wondrous effect. For this realism is not necessary; an entirely impressionistic and simplified design would serve the purpose. Horses and horsemen as well as warriors are indicated – roughly, it is true, but quite recognizably – on a few of the patterns visible on vases.

But Andromache's work was intended to be simpler: "She was decorating it with a floral pattern." We are not told if she was weaving this floral pattern or embroidering it. Both could have been possible. There might have been bands of something like woven honeysuckle, for the honeysuckle design was one of the most popular used for floral representation both on garments and in architecture. Perhaps it was a spot pattern with tiny flowerlets sprinkled over the ground at certain intervals; perhaps the flowers were embroidered in gold or silver thread. All these suggestions are possibilities.

We do know that quite complicated designs in weaving were carried out even by the young girls. There is a charming reference to the youthful and faulty efforts of Creusa at weaving in Euripides' *Ion*. It is one of the few detailed descriptions that we can find among the great dramatists' works of a decoration actually woven into a small garment. When the casket containing Ion's original baby clothes and trinkets is opened, Ion asks Creusa to describe them to him without her first seeing what is in the casket so that she can give him proof that she is his mother. The first thing that we are to understand is that, although they are richly decorated, they are woven. No hint of embroidery occurs in this description.

> *Creusa:* See the robe I wove when still a maid. *Ion:* What sort of a garment is it? For the loom of the virgin produces various woofs. *Creusa:* Not yet complete; it seems the work of inexperience. In the front of the garment is the Gorgon's head and the edge is decorated with serpents like the Aegis . . . a woof which my virgin shuttle made.

These designs that Euripides had in mind were in no way different from those described by Homer; in fact, this is a direct reference to the Aegis worn by Pallas Athene in the *Iliad* (see reference to Bk. V, *Iliad*). We therefore know that these same motifs were used throughout the centuries and, though it seems an unpleasant design to inflict upon a baby, it is completely in accordance with Homeric inspiration, and makes a traditional and dramatic point. The same passage goes on to describe the necklace that Ion had also worn as a baby. Here Euripides clearly indicates that it was because of their divine significance that such emblems were used for both fabrics and jewellery – to protect and influence the child.

> These . . . golden ornaments . . . fashioned in an antique style, with golden-cheeked dragons, Minerva's gift, who bids us rear our children amongst such forms, in imitation of our great Ericthonius . . . these, O my son, around his neck the new-born child should wear.

Before us we now have three distinct aspects of design, and all of them can be associated with the weaving of Greek fabrics. First, the fanciful and individually significant "Trojans and bronze-clad Achaeans", used as an expression of a personal problem of Helen's. Second, the floral pattern with which we can associate all the less significant forms, both floral and geometric, as old as Greece and permanently in use. Third, the divine symbols of the gods and goddesses. Roughly, Greek design can be divided into these three groups and the limitations are immediately apparent. And we cannot afford to disregard their dramatic significance.

It is sad that there are no known real paintings of the time to give us fuller insight into the variety of colours used in the patterns; the necessity to eliminate detail when painting on pottery has led to the designs being reduced to the very simplest. The motifs and running lines of pattern are similar, both in clothes and in architecture, and although in the study of classical architecture there seems to be an almost endless series of designs to remember with the complicated entablatures of the Ionic and Corinthian orders, these are limited very much by the space they have to decorate, and the same can be said of the decoration on clothes.

Most ornament was confined to bands of decoration. When all-over designs appear, they are in the form of spot patterns, squares, discs and ovals, or embroidered flower forms of the very simplest, which strictly eliminate every unnecessary leaf or petal that might confuse the design. Variations of the Greek key or scroll form appear more than anything else, but this might possibly be the fault of the artist whose job it was to decorate a vase freehand; these very simple ornaments were both quicker and safer to execute. Running borders of flower forms are frequently indicated; the famous honeysuckle and marigold and simple versions of the acanthus were the most popular forms of decoration for the garments of kings and queens and other noble persons. The architectural quality of the design is accentuated by the heavy folds of the material which, in so many instances, seem to imitate the fluting of the classic columns. There are examples of the use of animals in the most fascinating series of chain designs, and all the mythological beasts are there. Galloping horsemen, Pegasus, horses' heads, fighting warriors, sphinxes, harpies and sirens and other beasts or characters from the rich mythology of the time proceed in an endless procession around these bands of decoration. The simplicity of their silhouettes makes their subject matter a little difficult to see at first sight, but the effect is one of richness and vitality. The accompanying illustrations show the various ways in which these patterns were used, and the detailed examples of some of the motifs that were introduced should give the designer all possible information about the limitations of these ideas. Nearly all the examples depicted have been taken from the vases of the fifth and early fourth centuries B.C.; at a later date they are not nearly so interesting.

Colour is a comparatively easy subject to discuss, for already we know that there were foreign dyes and fabrics in use. The Egyptian range alone is wide, with all its beautiful earth dyes and the famous lapis-lazuli blue which was worth a king's ransom. The colour range from ancient Crete must still have been in use, for these were mostly the sea dyes; cuttle-fish blue and purple,

various seaweeds, and, of course, all the now-familiar vegetable dyes. One point
to be born in mind is that the woven woollen or linen fabrics were naturally
an off-white colour, so that they would normally take the dyes with a softness
similar to shantung and other Chinese silks. Pure white had to be bleached, and
it is doubtful if any bleaching process was used for a fabric that was going to be
dyed, for this was obviously not necessary. The bleaching process is a very
lengthy business without the aid of modern chemicals. As the colours produced
were much more sympathetic than modern chemical dyes, some care should
be taken in the selection of suitable colours so that brashness does not prevail.

Pollux has left us with a careful annotation of the colours that were used in
his time for certain types of characters. We are not at all certain that this is a
traditional or entirely acceptable scheme, but it is certainly worth some consideration. It is quite probable that colours had, by Pollux's time, come to signify certain qualities in certain people, but it is very unlikely that dramatists
adhered without question to a colour scheme that did not change with the
centuries. White occurs frequently in his list, and he tells us that the normal
costume for the tragic actor was a white Doric chiton with no seam on the
left side. He goes on to say that young men wore purple or red; old men
white, as did young women and priestesses. Parasites wore black or grey, old
women green or light blue. He is obviously not referring to the Greek drama,
for this list includes types characteristic of Roman comedy and not of fifth-
century drama.

Of these pastel shades mentioned by Pollux we have some considerable
evidence in the wall paintings of the first and second centuries A.D., also in the
little pots of ground colours which were taken from the house of the painter
at Pompeii and still exist in the Archaeological Museum at Naples. They are
pale, smoky shades, rather like a modern powder colour well mixed with white.
Certainly the pale blues, pinks and chromes are both varied and soft, and the
gorgeous vermilion walls in the House of the Mysteries show a rich purple-
madder and a deep chrome, perhaps one of the strongest of colour schemes, yet
beautifully dignified and restrained.

On the whole there seems to have been a magnificent range of colour, and the
only thing that is missing is the stridence of modern aniline dyes; but we still

have no proof that these were the colours used in the fifth century B.C. Homer mentions many colours, particularly purple, red and, occasionally, blue. There is, for example, the blue enamel on Agamemnon's cuirass (see p. 32), and the spindle of deep blue wool which Helen has had given her by Polybus who lived in Egyptian Thebes.

> Gifts . . . including a golden spindle and a basket that ran on castors and was made of silver finished with a rim of gold. This was the basket that her lady Phylo brought and set before her. It was full of fine spun yarn and the spindle with its deep blue wool was laid across it.

In the fifth century we find that whenever sheer splendour was required in dress, it is described in terms of colour. Brilliant colour had dramatic value. The description of the ghastly garment that Medea had sent to Creon's daughter (in *Medea* of Euripides) is variously described as "the splendid robe of a thousand dyes", "a garment finely wrought". Whatever the gown was supposed to look like it must have been outstandingly beautiful. For it is so splendid that the king's daughter, in spite of her very grave doubts about Medea's unexpectedly generous gesture and her natural reluctance to accept so fine a gift from such a famous sorceress, is tempted beyond her powers of resistance. The robe that Deianeira prepares with such loving care for the returning Heracles – unfortunately polluted by the same vicious type of poison – is described in the *Women of Trachis* by Sophocles in no less glowing terms as a thing of beauty and colour. These splendid garments of a thousand dyes have the same quality of magnificence and these glowing descriptions could very easily allude to the gorgeously decorated garments that appear on the vases supposed to represent dramatic characters (see p. 64). The dramatists often insist on black and sable as a sign of mourning; there is a particular point made of this in *Alcestis*, when Admetus proclaims that on the death of Alcestis the people must respect his sorrow; in this instance we are given quite clearly to understand that the characters did actually go off the scene and change both their masks and costumes. "I give command that all in solemn grief for this dear woman shear their locks and wear the sable garb of mourning".

It is remarkable that red should have been the colour that has always been connected with warriors even down to the redcoats in the century immediately behind us. The "crimson cloak of War" is mentioned more than once in classical drama, and one instance is of particular interest because the rather difficult problem of actual colour definition arises. In *Peace* of Aristophanes the author gives us a glimpse of the confusion between crimson and purple. "A cursed captain with his three plumes and his military cloak of startling crimson (he calls it true Sardian purple) which he takes care to dye himself with Cyzicus saffron in battle, then he is the first to run away shaking his plumes like a great yellow prancing cock". This tells us where two of the contemporary dyes come from, saffron from Cyzicus and the sea of Marmora, and purple from Sardis, one of the richest towns of the ancient world. This purple colour seems to have been nearer to magenta than to either purple or crimson, since there are early wall paintings that show this particular shade wherever the dress of royalty is indicated.

We are now nearing the end of our preliminary findings about fabrics, but there is one more fact of particular interest that must be mentioned before passing on to the main subject in hand – how these fabrics were worn. This is silk. It is not mentioned by Homer, probably for the very good reason that he had never seen it, but it is referred to many times in the works of both Euripides and Aristophanes, and such references are nearly always couched in the same terms, "transparent saffron gowns". In their time it was obviously something new and noticeable; a clinging transparent fabric straight from the golden cocoons of silkworms, its brilliant saffron colour immediately identifiable, making, as it must have done, a rich contrast to the more subtle earthy dyes normally in use.

This is the saffron robe worn by Dionysus in Euripides' *Bacchanals*; this is also the saffron robe referred to in *Lysistrata*, when Lysistrata and Calonice are swearing to entice and deny their menfolk. ". . . beautifully dressed in a saffron coloured robe . . . to the end that I may inspire my husband with the most ardent longings", and later in the same play these gowns are referred to as "sheet-anchors of our salvation . . . these saffron tunics, these scents and slippers, these cosmetics and transparent robes . . .". Now, silk straight from the silkworm is a brilliant yellow, clearer and warmer than saffron, although there may have been some added erotic significance attached to saffron itself, both its colour and its perfume. Aristophanes also mentions Amorgis silk which was famed for its transparent quality, and this would seem to be the forerunner of the cobweb silks that occur in so many fairy tales when many yards of such fabric must prove fine enough to be pulled through a ring taken from a king's finger.

We must not be inflexible about the actual construction of classic costume, but it is possible to find one or two governing factors that make the whole problem easier to understand. Generally speaking, classic costume as worn from the Attic period until the time of the Roman Empire was comparatively sim-

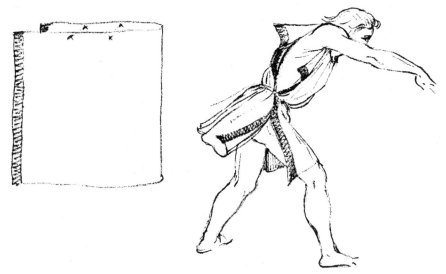

Fig. 2. Doric chiton without fold

ple, although there is a rich variety of superficial small garments that tend to complicate the general effect. The accepted terms of definition applied to the *chiton*, or main dress, are Doric and Ionic; this divides them according to two of the main orders in architecture, which were developed by the two leading racial groups, Ionian Greeks and Dorian Greeks. The Doric was severely simple; the Ionic a trifle more complicated, as indeed the Ionic is in every sense.

Taking the Doric chiton first, we find that it was a straight, unsewn piece of material, wrapped around the body and pinned on the shoulders. The material could be of almost any width, from a yard up to about three yards, but it was probably not wider than three yards (see Fig. 2).

The width of the woven material formed the line from neck to hem, and the length of the material went round the body. Therefore, the wider the fabric

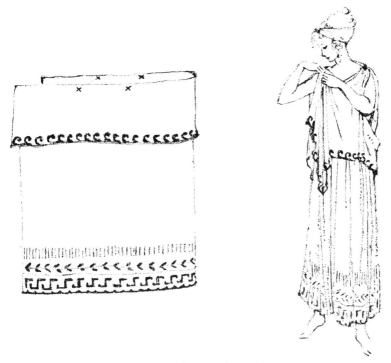

Fig. 3. Doric chiton with top fold

the longer the gown. Thus whenever Homer mentions "double-width" he means that the robe was luxuriously long, possibly even trailing on the ground. The method of wearing it differed only in the adjustment of the width to suit the wearer. If the material is folded in half and two pins inserted half a yard from either end, the head can then be put through the space between the pins and the chiton will fall from the shoulders suspended by the pins, open at the right side with a folded loop under the left arm (see Fig. 2). A girdle holds the garment in position. This is the simplest form and is worn by working and fighting men and sometimes by serving women. The more usual feminine,

Fig. 4. Two different arrangements of the Doric chiton

decorative style is to fold over the top of the chiton before inserting the pins so that a hanging drapery falls from the pins and shows the (probably decorated) top or border of the material hanging over the chest like a collar.

The placing of the girdle is an entirely personal matter. Should the chiton be very long, which fashion normally occurs for women only, there may be two girdles worn, one high up under the breasts, and one at the waist. The extra material swags out under the lower girdle. Generally speaking, the Doric version is simple. The pins were long and pointed like little daggers with a decorated end. Apparently they were, on occasion, used as such, and served in emergencies as small weapons of defence.

Fig. 5. Ionic chiton

The Ionic chiton is much fuller than the Doric (i.e. the material has the same width but is longer), and is sewn up like a vast unshaped skirt. To put it on, one of the open edges should be pinned at regular intervals leaving a slightly larger interval for the head to go through. The hands are then put through between the last pin at each end and the fold in the fabric. This will form a sort of long sleeve with the pins decorating the arm and permitting the material to fall open between them, showing the bare arm. About five yards of length is required to give the right effect (see Figs. 5 & 7). Again, it can be girdled as desired. The girdle itself will help to pleat the skirt.

Care should be exercised in the choice of fabrics used; we can assume that the majority of these chitons were originally made from very fine wool. This would give them the full beauty of the softly flowing draperies. The easiest type of modern fabric with which to experiment is a fine jersey type which, because of its weight, falls much better than any sort of cotton or than most of the synthetic fabrics.

These Ionic chitons were frequently pleated. The pleating could have been done in a manner similar to broomstick pleating, which is still the most economical method of pleating real silk. The silk is folded tightly when wet and wound around a straight stick till it is dry; when dry, the pleats remain in place until the material is washed again. This could only be done with a perfectly straight length of material with no flares or cutting on the cross because of the stretching involved. If this very simple method had been used in the fifth century it would account for the arrangement of groups of little pleats, and again groups of larger ones, a form which is so very effective in the clear calligraphic drawings on Greek vases.

No doubt many of the lovely drawings that fascinate one by their pleated fantasy were not so exaggerated as we might believe from looking at them.

Fig. 6. Theseus

One little figure in the British Museum showing Theseus slaying the Minotaur has fascinated me for many years because of the pleated magnificence of his chiton (see drawing above). Because of this figure an experiment in broomstick pleating was carried out. A length of material about six yards long and forty-two inches wide was used. When this came off the broom it was easy to handle. The top could be turned down over a cord arranged around the shoulders, and after a deal of fiddling it was discovered that as long as there was sufficient material, the chevron edge could be achieved and pinned into place on the cord, so that however much movement was carried out the hemline

Fig. 7. Ionic chiton and himation; Doric chiton sewn up at side

remained the same, fuller wherever it was lifted than at its deeper points. The Greek artists boggled at the detailed drawing of the complicated pleated fold around the cord and under the arms. In their simplified rendering such a fold is turned into what appears to us to be some separate edge. Possibly the same effect could be achieved from a length of material with both sides chevroned, but there would not be the same depth and variety of fold on the lifted or dropped hem.

It is difficult for us to realize that experiment in hanging and drapery was of more interest to the Greek artists than just making use of a piece of material and turning up a hem, as we are prone to do. The lesson might be learned from them that hems are a nuisance and that a properly woven selvage edge, as long as the material is not too diaphanous, must be straight. It is also probable that weights were used to assist the correct hanging of some of these garments. We know that such weights, designed as tassels or drops, decorate the points of himations, also that fringe, the natural finish to any length of woven material, appears on quite a number of garments. The pleated edge which is left free between the pins or brooches down the shoulders makes a lovely serrated scallop pattern which also looks most attractive in the drawings but would set a real problem for a designer who wished to reproduce such an effect.

A description of what sounds uncommonly like an Ionic chiton can be found in Book XVIII of the *Odyssey*, when Penelope is brought gifts from her suitors. Whether this particular gown was known in Homer's time is debatable, but this indicates so very clearly something of the sort that it would seem to fit very well and might have been a copyist's idea: ". . . For Antinous they brought a long embroidered robe of the most beautiful material on which were fixed a dozen golden brooches, each fitted with a curved sheath for the pin". The twelve golden brooches would seem to be the six pins which appear on each arm. These pins were sheathed, an important improvement on the original dagger type of pin; they were also already on the robe, so that in a sense it was made up and therefore a finished garment ready to wear.

When putting on the chiton care should be taken that the main fullness is at the front and at the back; not at the sides. This arrangement gives the hips a clean smooth line, leaving the folds at the front and back to swing gracefully from the girdle when moving, and to hang in a series of straight lines when standing still.

The upper part, above the girdle, should be lifted at the sides until the "hemline" is even and then swagged over the girdle under the arms. Normally if the material is sufficiently soft and weighty this will give an effective series of V-shaped folds on the chest pulling from the pins on the shoulders and accentuating a slightly clinging effect on the breasts only. This obviously was the fashionable contour to be achieved by women.

The normal male form of Ionic chiton is short, with perhaps only two or three pins on each shoulder so that the sleeve rarely reaches the elbow. When men wear the full style already described it would seem that its use in illustration was to define special characters. Either the man is elderly, inactive or regal, or else the figure represents the god Dionysus, who is so frequently accused of being feminine. Therefore we may assume that the Doric form is the more masculine.

One instance only appears when this garment is adapted so that it may serve a more practical purpose than that possible when pins are used; this occurs when, instead of the pins on each shoulder, a strap or band of embroidery is sewn on the left side connecting the front to the back, leaving a folded swag under the left arm and completely freeing the right side down to the waist where the garment is held in place by a belt or girdle. Such an arrangement is used when warriors are shown in action, and this appears on both relief figures as well as paintings. It is worn by both men and Amazons and was quite obviously a form of battledress.

Over the chiton was worn a cloak some four or five yards long and about a yard in width. This is known as an *himation* and was arranged and decorated in a variety of styles. The ends were decorated and quite often had a fringe or tassels or some small weight of beads attached at the corners, so that in movement the weight swung away from the body and emphasized the pattern of the border design. It was worn, as all the garments were, by both men and women. There was no distinctive garment peculiar to either sex, though a version of the himation with the lower edge woven in points and the upper edge pleated on to a band worn under one arm and fastened on the opposite shoulder seems to appear far more frequently on women than it does on men. This highly decorative pleated himation is nearly always represented as one of Athene's garments, also those of queens and other noble women. Its shape lends itself readily to sculpture and the borders of decoration make a fine pattern on the figured vases. When the himation is worn with the chevron edge the pleating

Fig. 8. Noble women with diadems, Ionic chitons and draped himations

at once becomes something of a mystery. Various views have been expressed as to the exact way in which this was attached to the band at the top. Such a band was arranged from one shoulder, across the breast and under the other arm and back to the shoulder again. The himation was attached to this and was fastened with a row of pins down the arm in much the same manner as the Ionic chiton. The effect was both graceful and decorative, for the points hanging from the arm seem to have been weighted so that they were dragged straight in movement. These himations are always pleated although the pleats do not appear to be pressed. Sometimes the whole length resembled an accordion pleating in that each pleat was exactly the same distance away from its neighbour; at other times a cluster of little pleats seems to have been attached at certain intervals to the band that encircles the body. In many cases the top of the pleated material is free and folds over the band in a series of decorative scallops (see p. 28). It appears that these himations are arranged with geometrical care. The arrangement is similar to the cartridge pleating used in the time of Henry VIII, when vast amounts of woollen fabric were folded into regularly spaced loops and each loop left free. From both drawings and sculpture it looks as if the place where the attachment was made was some five or six inches from the top edge of the material.

Fig. 9. Full himation

If, as is so often the case, the material had a border, this border would hang down over the band forming the decorative scallops already referred to above. The chevron edge is also decorated with some sort of design, not necessarily similar to that at the top.

There are literally dozens of different arrangements of the himation, and it would seem impossible to lay down any definite laws as to the exact shape and manner in which it is worn on some of the sculptured figures. Probably many of the lovely, intricate draperies show artistic licence, and the curious manner in which such draperies flow defies a practical analysis.

The normal purpose of the himation or great-cloak was as a protection from the elements, so that during the winter the himation became as valuable to the Greeks as the plaid to a Scotsman, and the whole figure can be swathed in its voluminous folds.

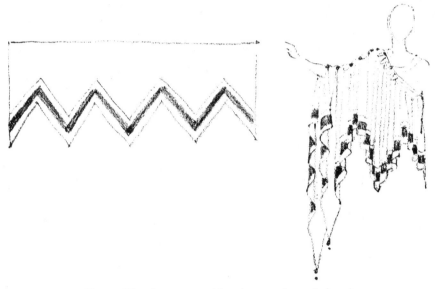

Fig. 10. Himation woven with a chevron edge and pleated

Yet another form of cloak is the *chlamys*, a short and generally much briefer affair, which is sometimes shown tied round the body under one arm and round the waist, or just buckled on one shoulder, the ends falling straight. The chlamys was used chiefly by soldiers and messengers.

One more garment which had various uses was known as the *peplos*. This could have been a tunic woven straight on the loom in the manner already described, but there are obvious examples which look as if they were made up with a shoulder seam and embroidered neckband. The difficulty is that often some such neckbands, holding the pleats or gathers in place, appear also on the chiton. For the sake of clarity in description, I shall use the word "peplos" whenever the garment is obviously made up. This is a perfectly adequate term for the little tunics that are worn over a chiton for warmth or decoration, and it can also apply to many of the tunics that are worn by servants and fighting men. It can be made with or without sleeves (Fig. 32 & Fig. 28 right).

This inventory, then, completes the fundamental garments with which we are concerned. Other foreign tunics, and some of the more extraordinary examples of clothing, will be discussed later.

It will be seen that the chief variations in dress can be obtained by the use of a combination of two or more garments, each decorated differently and having borders that fall in a different manner. Materials woven in oblong lengths were used to their fullest purpose to display the perfection of bordered folds.

Basically, we now have the structure of Greek classic costume before us and can appreciate the fact that one of its more important limitations is its squareness and architectural quality. It has been said that the main difference between Greek and Roman ways of expression was based on the fact that where the Greeks used right-angles and straight lines, the Romans used curves. However literally such an analysis is taken, the fact remains that the Greek himation did have square ends and the Roman toga was based on a circle or semicircle. We need not go farther than this.

We have now reached a stage where all our designs should be governed by

Fig. 11. Pleated, stitched himation

Fig. 12. Three views of figure wearing himation for warmth

Fig. 13. Shepherd

a few very simple rules, the same rules that governed the Greeks. The main consideration, then, was a length of material and how to use it to its fullest advantage without cutting it up or wasting any of it.

CHAPTER II

Armour

Homer's splendid descriptions of the grandeur of the archaic warrior inspired not only the dramatists but also the artists who illustrated his legends throughout the centuries that came after. Therefore we find that, to a certain extent, our problems of bridging the gap between archaic legend and the dramatic heroes of the fifth century are solved. Presumably the artists who painted scenes from the *Iliad* followed the written word as much as they were able, translating such descriptions into forms and silhouettes which they themselves understood. This fact is particularly obvious in the descriptions of fighting men and, apart from the fanciful details of Achilles' magic armour designed and made by the lame god Hephaestus (*Iliad*, Bk. XVIII), such descriptions can be made to tally with the majority of the vital little figures decorating fifth-century pottery. In such passages where the dramatists describe the armour, the full force of Homer's example has been followed. Particularly is this so in *Seven against Thebes*, which I shall quote later in this chapter.

Suppose first of all we take as an example the complete armour as worn by Agamemnon (*Iliad*, Bk. II); we can identify each piece as something we have seen in the paintings. Such an exercise is very necessary because we are not in this instance interested in the real archaic, but in how the actors of the fifth century appeared.

Agamemnon's armour is described in the following glowing terms:

. . . himself put on his gleaming bronze. He began by tying round his legs a pair of splendid greaves which were fitted with silver clips for the ankles. Next, he put on his breast the cuirass that Cinyras had once presented to him as a friendly gift. News had reached Cinyras in far off Cyprus of the great Achaean expedition that was sailing to Troy, and he had sent the cuirass as a gracious offering to the king. It was made of parallel strips, ten dark blue enamel, twelve of gold and twenty of tin. On either side three snakes rose up in coils towards the opening of the neck. Their iridescent enamel made them look like the rainbow that the son of Cronos

32

hangs on a cloud as a portent to mankind below. Next, Agamemnon slung his sword from his shoulders. Golden studs glittered on the hilt, but the sheath was of silver, with a golden baldric attached. Then he took up his manly and man-covering shield, a nobly decorated piece, with its ten concentric rings of bronze and twenty knobs of tin making a white circle around the dark enamel boss. The central figure on it was a grim, gorgon's head with awe-compelling eyes, and on either side of her, Panic and Rout were depicted. It was fitted with a golden baldric round which a writhing snake of blue enamel twisted the three heads that grew from a single neck. On his head Agamemnon put his helmet with its four plates, its double crest and its horsehair plume nodding defiantly above.

All these motifs are shown on the armour of the fifth and even the fourth centuries B.C. Naturally there is never quite so much detail in the vase painting, for simplicity is the keynote of their design, but the stripes of enamel are clearly indicated on many of the breastplates. The shield with its rings of bronze and white studding around the edge is a sort of standard pattern that forms the framework for the central boss with its emblem of an eye, a gorgon's head, snakes or some more complicated and defiant blazon (Fig. 14).

Aeschylus describes the shields in his *Seven against Thebes* with Homeric detail, and that the body of Polynices is brought in from the battlefield at the end of this play. In all probability his shield must make an appearance. The description of this is particularly interesting. "His new-wrought orbed shield he holds, with a double impress charged: a warrior, blazing all in golden arms, a female form of modern aspect expressing justice, the inscription reads – 'Yet once more to this country, and once more to his paternal Throne, I will restore him.'" Presumably such an inscription was written around the rim of the outer shield. The other shields described are well worth considering, although they do not necessarily appear in the theatre. "On his proud shield portrayed, a naked man waves in his hand a blazing torch; beneath in golden letters, 'I will fire the city.'" Another describes "A man in armour his ladder fixed against the enemy's walls, most resolute to rend the rampires down; . . . the blazon speaks 'Not Mars himself shall beat me from the tower.'" Aeschylus particularly mentions that all these shields are sculptured so that we know the motifs are raised up and not painted.

The *Phoenician Women* of Euripides also gives us an assortment of descriptive detail about armour. Such characters do not appear on the stage, but the

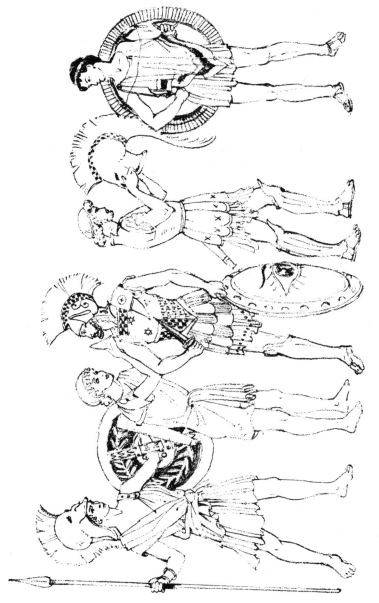

Fig. 14. Greek fighting men, 5th cent. B.C.

Phoenician women describe what they see: "... a multitude in burnished armour", "... his shield with stars is covered...", "... arrayed in particoloured mail, half barbarian...", "... how gracefully in golden arms arrayed, bright as Hyperion's radiant beams he moves...", "... on his left arm the Hydra with a hundred snakes begirt, which filled the convex surface of

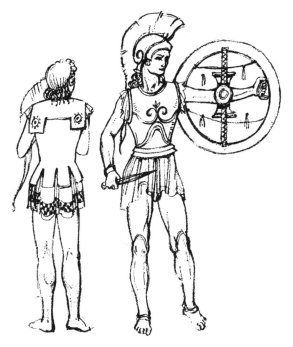

Fig. 15. Backview of shoulder-pieces and handgrip on shield

his shield, that badge of Argive pride the warrior loose from Thebes", and one other reference to the large, man-covering shield, "... ascending, still sufficient shelter found beneath the huge circumference of his shield". Armour in the fifth century, B.C., though primarily made as a protection to the body, was also used as a method of impressing and frightening an enemy. The persistence of fear and the cold nightmare of pursuit which appear on Athene's aegis are here again in the emblems carried by warriors. That the armour was of wonderful workmanship was obvious.

The shields were hollowed out with a deep curve so that any blow struck

Fig. 16. Greek warriors, Corinthian on left, from the Siphnian Treasury

on the outside would be at least six inches away from the body and only in the centre where the arm supported it was there any real danger from penetration. There are references to a spy-hole in the centre of the shield. The hollow is referred to in Aristophanes' *Acharnians*: "Pack the rugs in the hollow of the targe". This made a useful holdall when on manœuvres.

Normally the shields were made from either leather or bronze or plain ox-hide stretched on a bronze frame, studded with bronze or tin. The inside had great leather straps and handholds. There are many references to the ox-hide being seven layers thick. There were two different sizes normally in use, the great shield, "man-covering", which could completely cover the body if the owner were crouching behind, and the target shield referred to as "targe" which was used as craftily as possible and required a great deal of skill and agility in order to manœuvre it strategically in battle. Its great advantage was that it was both light and easy to wield.

The *cuirass*, or breastplate, as described as the gift of Cinyras, is a perfect example of the breastplates illustrated in battle scenes on many vases. Stripes and checks of enamel or some other contrasting metallic ornament appear far more frequently than animals. It is impossible to say definitely that one cuirass was made of leather and another of bronze, although there is some pretty clear indication in some of the pictures that a metal breastplate supports the apron below. The figures at Delphi that decorated the Siphnian treasury give the impression of leather, the manner in which the tassets are flared out from the hips without any defining line might make one think that they were separate and came from underneath. The form of the shoulder-pieces is, however, in this instance almost identical with the drawings of what looks like bronze armour on the red figured vases of a century or so later. Yet at the same time either of these examples could have been inspired by Homer's description of Athene protecting Menelaus.

> With her own hand she guided the piercing dart . . . to where the golden buckles of the belt were fixed and the corslet overlapped. So that the sharp arrow struck the fastened belt and pressed on through the ornate cuirass, and through the apron that Menelaus wore as a last protection against flying weapons. This did more than the rest to save him as the arrow sped on through the apron too. Eventually it made a shallow wound. . . .

Menelaus says that "it was stopped by the metal of my belt, the corslet underneath and the apron with the bronze they put upon it". Here we are given to understand that this apron was made by the coppersmiths and was probably a series of flaps (or tassets as they were called in later armour) hanging from the waist or under the belt and the cuirass.

The famous mosaic in Naples Museum of Alexander in battle with the Persians shows his cuirass as one still with a colourful design, probably modelled

Fig. 17. Two Greek warriors and (at right) an Asiatic or mercenary

on ideas as extravagant as those described by Homer for Agamemnon some five hundred years earlier. The gorgon's head, in this instance, is quite easily discernible and obviously some quite complicated pattern is intended. One peculiarity of the Greek cuirass is that there appear to be thongs holding the shoulder-pieces in position. These thongs sometimes are crossed over the front and tied at the waist, sometimes they seem to be attached by little bows to some hidden ring or hole on the chest; again there are several examples where the thongs are tied straight down to the waist without crossing.

One other point is of interest to the designer or producer, and that is the reference to "Agamemnon slinging his sword from his shoulders"; interesting, because, at a later date, when armour was worn, the sword was attached to a sword-belt and worn below the waist. The Greek soldier is rarely shown wearing a sword at all, but when he does it hangs from a strap across the cuirass and not from the waist. It was a very short sword and worn practically at breast height so that the scabbard or sheath could be held in place by the left arm whilst the sword was drawn with the right hand at elbow height. These swords seem rarely to have been more than eighteen inches in length. The Greeks were primarily spearsmen; the short sword was carried for close fighting only for, obviously, no long sword could be carried in this manner. They seem to have been the only warriors in history who carried the sword slung across the chest.

The helmets of beaten bronze were as decorative as imagination could make them. The varieties used to decorate vases and adorn the heads of sculptured warriors are well worth some careful study. The Corinthian helmet was, perhaps, the most awe-inspiring, for it was made with a complete cover for the face, with a hook-like nose-piece, elongated chin and a curved neck-piece. It is often shown worn on the back of the head with the whole of the face looking rather like a gruesome skull on the top of the head. The plumes that decorate this particular form of helmet would seem to be all horsehair, but there is a fine sweep at the back which normally curls away from the shoulders and must have been supported by some form of stiffening that did not impede the movement of the wearer. The Attic helmet was much smaller though more highly decorated. It had hinged cheek-pieces or plates which could be pushed up to look almost like upstanding ears, and the plumes normally ran only in a stiff semicircle over the head without the long tail behind. The head-piece was always decorated, possibly with the personal emblem of the wearer but more probably a design worked by the hands of some imaginative bronze-worker. The same familiar decorations of flowers, animals and figures and those mythical monsters inseparable from the art of the age are there. Sometimes the decoration is geometric, a chess-board check, fish scales or just a plain studding. The helmets worn by the Thracians were similar to these, but the plumes seem to

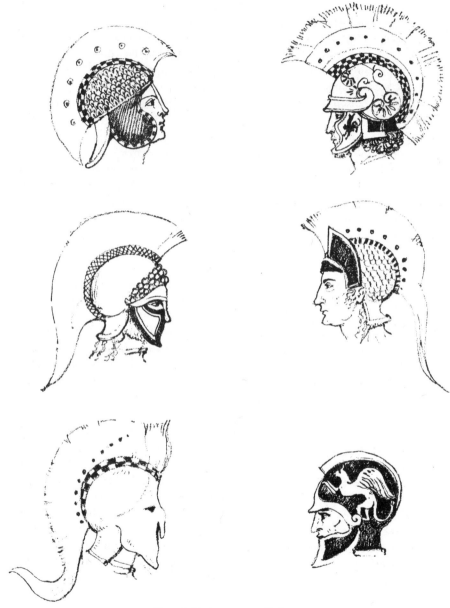

Fig. 18. Various types of helmet

be softer and not necessarily dyed horsehair. The head-piece itself is more of a snail shape with a hinged eye-piece sculptured with a relief design of curls around the forehead. The supporting structure for the plumes is always decorated with some geometric pattern incised or embossed or possibly enamelled. The actual specimens of the real bronze helmets which still exist are, naturally, without their plumes, but traces of designs can be distinctly seen and indentations mark the places which may have been used for the introduction of enamel or contrasting metals.

Their purpose was twofold, to terrify and protect. Here, for instance, is the passage from *Iliad*, Bk. VI, in which Hector frightens his small son with the waving plumes of his helmet.

> The glorious Hector held out his arms to take his boy. But the child shrank back with a cry to the bosom of his girdled nurse, alarmed by his father's appearance. He was frightened by the bronze helmet and the horsehair plume that he saw nodding grimly down at him. . . . But noble Hector quickly took his helmet off and put the dazzling thing on the ground.

For purposes of comparison I have included Figure 19 illustrating Roman armour. Of one thing we are quite certain, and that is that the armour in ancient Greece was utterly unlike that of the Roman soldier. Greek breastplates were hinged or buckled with silver buckles or tied with thongs. They were not made to follow the form of the body but to repel a spear-thrust by presenting a smooth surface. They fitted on to the shoulders with shoulder-pieces which always fastened in front. The neck was high in front but higher still at the back, and the back of the neck was also covered by the protective neck-piece on the back of the helmet. A wide belt was worn under the cuirass and from this the apron was suspended. By this I mean the apron as described by Homer (see p. 37). Under this a leather one was sometimes worn. Greaves of bronze or other metal were worn by many, but these were not necessary. There are many pictures of bare-footed Greek soldiers, also some who have only partial armour such as a breastplate or corslet worn over a chiton, or merely a helmet or a shield.

A delightfully decorative form of dress appears in the vase paintings and in one or two sculptured figures which represent archers or fighting men from almost any country other than Greece itself. For lack of a better definition this is usually referred to as Asiatic costume. Amazons and Persians are often shown

Fig. 19. Roman cuirasses from Olympia Museum

wearing it. It could well represent the type of dress described in *Iliad*, Bk. X, that the Trojan, Dolan, son of Eumides, one of the sacred heralds, donned when he volunteered to run to the ships and spy out the land, "who at once slung his curved bow on his shoulders, threw the pelt of a grey wolf over it, adjusted a ferret-skin cap on his head, and picking up a sharp javelin set out from the camp". Fundamentally, it appears to be a pair of skin-fitting ballet tights without feet, and a leotard, both decorated with amusing variety (see illustration Fig. 20). These garments may have been made of wool or of soft leather. They obviously gave complete freedom of movement to the wearer. An animal's skin or a chiton or a peplos could be worn over them. The helmets that go with this dress are of leather (ferret-skin?) and have hanging flaps in front of the ears and a protective covering at the back. In the central figure seen below the pattern appears rather like the slashings on Elizabethan garments. This would lead us to believe that in this instance, at least, the garments were made of some kind of skin. Whatever the fabrics used, they were obviously both warm and useful as

Fig. 20. Three archers wearing Asiatic costume

well as being highly decorative. Shepherds are sometimes depicted as wearing the same sort of under-dress, with their himations or peplos worn over it. Obviously this was for warmth as the Greek winters are extremely cold (Fig. 13).

Sometimes shoes are worn but frequently the leg-covering is secured by a strap or heel-piece under the foot, which leaves the toes uncovered. The desire for pattern extends to the armour, such as it is. Both the quiver and the shield are of unusual design. The shield is quite different from the Greek shield, being quite often a crescent shape or an oval.

The lid to a beautiful bronze bowl in the British Museum is decorated with four little archers of this type, presumably Amazons from Campania, a state

Fig. 21. Amazons from bronze bowl in British Museum, c. 500 B.C.

of western Italy roughly in the area of Naples. The date of this elegant and detailed example is about 500 B.C. Each of these figures is in a slightly different position, sitting on horseback in various stages of shooting or loading their bows. The costume is similar in each case, although one figure at least has an elbow-length sleeve. It is skin-tight from throat to ankle and bears indications of some minute pattern. A tight belt at the waist supports a decorative little apron at the back; there appears to be a band of embroidery or decoration just above the elbow and in two of the figures this occurs again at the wrist. A sort of knee-cap also is indicated, though this is uncertain, as it might possibly be a knee-length sock coming up over the thigh covering. The feet are bare and the hair is worn in long curls at the back and neater ones on the forehead. The caps are conical, rather similar to a Phrygian cap but with an opening at the top or peak. The quiver is attached on the right side of the neck to the cap itself by a wide band fixed round the head; this also is decorated. It would seem probable that the knee-cap, or what appears to be a knee-cap, was worn to save the knee from galling as no saddle or stirrup is visible, and the archers seem to be riding bareback (see opposite).

CHAPTER III

Insignia of gods and goddesses

Emblems and insignia were of the greatest significance to all the Greek artists. To us, in an age when heraldry has lost its value, this once important means of identification carries little weight. Not so to the Greeks. Mythology had woven golden skeins of folk-lore around every heraldic motif used to symbolize each deity, and the design varied according to the education of the various artists concerned. Here lies an opportunity for design which could be used to great advantage in the theatre. Perhaps one should enlarge on this.

The warlike insignia peculiar to Zeus and Athene was the *aegis*. Its development historically is particularly interesting for its origins are most primitive, yet we find Homer described it in such glowing detail that its magnificence inspired artists throughout the ages to come.

During the archaic period the aegis was represented as a skin hanging from the left arm and tied round the neck, thus forming a shield. This seems to have been the earliest type of primitive shield for the body and appears in various reliefs and designs at a time when the shield itself had developed into a highly efficient piece of decorative armour. There is a figure of Heracles in the famous Sicyonian Frieze at Delphi (sixth century B.C.) which clearly shows how the hind legs of the animal were tied on one shoulder – its body and front legs hanging from the left arm and the head forming a protective covering for the left hand (see Fig. 22). Tradition, vacillating as it does around the various myths and legends, has it that the skin was a goat's skin, but the bloodthirsty brutality of primitive legend also describes it as the Gorgon's skin flayed by Athene from this miserable wretch. It is unnecessary to plunge deeper into the dozens of stories that spring from or are associated with the aegis, but this particular myth sticks, in the sense that the Gorgon's head with its halo of serpents nearly always appears as part of the "cloak".

Pallas Athene, preparing for war in the *Iliad*, Bk. V, is said to have shed her soft embroidered robe, which she had made with her own hands, put

46

Fig. 22. Pallas Athene from bronze in Athens Museum and Heracles (or Zeus) from Siphnian
Treasury

on a tunic in its place, and equipped herself for the lamentable work of war with the arms of Zeus the Cloud-compeller. She threw around her shoulders the formidable tasselled aegis, which is beset at every point with Fear, and carries Strife and Force and the cold nightmare of Pursuit within it, and also bears the ghastly image of a Gorgon's head, the grim and redoubtable emblem of aegis-bearing Zeus. On her head she put her golden helmet, with its four plates and double crest, adorned with fighting men of a hundred towns. . . .

An earlier description (Bk. II) runs in a softer vein:

Athene of the Flashing Eyes, wearing her splendid cloak, the unfading everlasting aegis, from which a hundred golden tassels flutter, all beautifully made, each worth a hundred heads of cattle. . . .

The two descriptions do not exactly tally, which makes them all the more interesting, for the one endows it with a nightmare quality and enlarges upon its formidable aspect whilst the other gives it supreme rarity and beauty. The reference to the tassels means the snakes of gold that hang from the edge of the skin. In many representations this skin is scalloped and each scallop is decorated with a single small snake, its head entwined with the tail of the next one. Fear, Strife and Force are also supposed to be indicated by these same snakes; the snake has always been an emblem of fear as well as having a connexion with the underworld, and the Strife is taking place between the entwined snakes. All three of these savage emotions are expressed in the Gorgon's head.

From the sixth century B.C. onwards, almost any of the pictured or sculptured Athenes could easily have been taken from either or both of these descriptions from Homer.

During the fifth century B.C., however, the aegis gradually begins to change its shape and even its texture. In the earlier examples it is always recognizable as a skin of leather, but now there are instances where it is quite distinctly a collar, not necessarily made of leather any longer but having the scaled texture of a fish or overlapping scaled armour. This is still decorated with fearsome snakes but even these are beginning to lose their identity as snakes and are often shown as a series of question-marks hanging from the serrated edge of the collar. The gorgon's head is embossed on the front of the collar. The whole meaning of the original aegis is lost although it remains a distinguishing emblem peculiar to the

Fig. 23. Pallas Athene with Corinthian helmet and aegis of leopard-skin, and (right) with Attic helmet and scaled aegis

Fig. 24. Pallas Athene showing three different ways of representing helmets and aegis

goddess. Eventually, by the beginning of the fourth century, we see it as a mere shadow of its former horrific self, a collar or even a necklace of question-marks.

All these variations appear more or less simultaneously during the fifth century. It was in all probability a matter of artistic whim, which, if any, of the appropriate insignia should be introduced into any particular design. Some artists obviously copy from an earlier work, whilst others seek to be as modern and simplified as they dare and use an absolute minimum of detail to give the impression that they want. There are instances where certain artists prefer to leave out both the gorgon's head and the snakes; this is particularly noticeable in the beautiful bronze figure of Athene in the museum at Athens (see Fig. 22).

Athene's helmet so impressively described in the passage already quoted rarely bears any similarity to this early description. In fact, it often takes on the characteristics of the district, where the artist may find in local forms the example he is seeking; only rarely do we see it with the double crest – two crests mounted side by side on the top of the helmet. The famous figure carved by Phidias (illustrated in the accompanying drawing, Fig. 25) showed not only two crests but three, the centre one mounted higher, the cheek-pieces or plates hinged up in the form of horns beside the triple crest. The "fighting men of a hundred cities" would be a heavy undertaking for any artist and an isolated example carved by some specialist in detail would be the exception and not the rule. Examples of Corinthian, Attic and Thracian helmets are all worn by Athene and appear in vase paintings and in sculpture; more familiar, perhaps, are those pictures or bronzes that show the plume mounted on a swan's neck or a curved form like a question-mark which lifts the plume far up above the head, adding

Fig. 25. Three-crested helmet

Fig. 26. Hermes and Heracles

height to the figure of this all-powerful virgin goddess. She also carries a spear. So much for Athene.

Hermes as a messenger conforms to the classic idea that all messengers are travellers and must therefore wear boots and a hat. Instead of the traveller's staff he carries the *caduceus* which was originally a staff with heraldic white streamers at its tip. At some stage in its development these streamers were mistaken for snakes, possibly a natural error, for Hermes was the herald to Hades, and snakes, as I have already said, were considered an emblem of the unseen world. This form was general by the fifth century, and the caduceus is normally shown as two serpents in a figure of eight surmounted by a pair of wings. The wings are important, for Hermes was appointed by Zeus as his herald and, according to tradition, given the staff, a round hat against the rain, also with wings, and winged golden sandals which carried him with the swiftness of the wind. We can see the odd results once again of one artist copying from another without perhaps realizing the full meaning of the emblems he was using, for during the fifth century frequently the caduceus is found reduced to a form that for all the world looks like a pair of pincers mounted on a stick. The hat varies considerably, for though tradition says it should be round, the artist saw it as a hat familiar to himself; the wings were added with no particular bird in mind. Thus we get hats of almost every shape and sometimes even helmets. The same with the boots, which vary from a flimsy sandal with tiny wings at the heel to a really impressive boot decorated with fur or skin just below the knee, and carrying some intricate design embossed upon the calf with great wings growing from ankle to knee.

Dionysus also presents us with a number of problems both interesting and confusing, for the myths surrounding this god of wine, madness, festivity and tragedy obviously had much to do with the manner in which he is depicted and the character which he assumes in the theatre. Normally in decoration he is represented as wearing a flowing beard, his head wreathed in ivy or vine-leaves, his hair long and curled in the tight corkscrew ringlets dear to the hearts of archaic artists. Sometimes the hair is done up at the back or even tied back at the nape of the neck, but more often it flows unbound and unrestrained apart from the wreath of leaves or some other type of fillet. Supposedly disguised in his youth as a girl to escape the anger of Hera, he seems to have acquired feminine tastes and elegances in his manner of dress ever after. This peculiarity

Fig. 27. Hermes and Dionysus

was made a source of ridicule in at least two of the plays in which he appears; Aristophanes' *Frogs* and Euripides' *Bacchanals*. In the latter we may suppose that Dionysus was still unbearded, for Pentheus, King of Thebes, accuses him of effeminacy and says in anger " . . . thy dainty tresses will I cut off", to which Dionysus replies, "Hallowed my locks are, fostered by the gods." Then Pentheus says, "Next yield me thy Thyrsus from thy hands", and Dionysus replies, "This is Dionysus' wand." This wand is as variable as the caduceus of Hermes and appears in many shapes. It is usually shown wreathed in ivy leaves, for the Greek ivy leaf was considered as an intoxicant and was supposedly chewed by the followers of Dionysus to provoke them to ecstasy. It is variously described – as a fennel stalk with ivy leaves growing out of it, as an ivy-twined staff with a cluster of pine cones on the top, and as a three-branched fennel with the centre flower higher than its two companions. It is drawn as a stiff wand and as a wavy one, also as a waving branch with various types of leaf growing out of it. It can be a plain staff too without the head of leaves or cones. On many vases Dionysus is just waving a branch of some highly decorative design; this may or may not have been intended to represent the Dionysiac wand, for such pictures could be examples of the ecstatic chase when branches and small animals were torn up in the mad pursuit of vernal ecstasy. Besides or instead of the *thyrsus* Dionysus carries a jug or great drinking bowl of wine in many of his representations; he also wears a faun-skin tied round his shoulders or even made up into a tunic-like garment (see Fig. 27). This faun-skin is not always discernible as such, in fact artists indicate it in many ways.

Dionysus also seems to specialize in transparent garments. There is no doubt in the modern mind that these transparent flowing garments are feminine, for they are constructed with groups of pleats so that in movement they cling to the figure, but "feminine" and "masculine" are difficult to define in the history of costume. At almost any given period men and women have accused each other of stealing costume characteristics from the opposite sex. The Greeks were no exceptions to this. Because Dionysus sported a clinging saffron robe he immediately becomes the butt for contemporary humour. He also wears *buskins* which are considered feminine. These boots have soft-footed soles with a slightly turned-up toe vaguely reminiscent of the boots worn by the Assyrians, and purposely turned up to add speed to movement in the sand. Pictures of Dionysus frequently show him wearing these boots and it would seem that this is the type of boot worn by a female chorus, though few of the fifth-century illustrations show us women wearing any sort of boot at all. There are one or two examples, however, of chorus dressing, one particularly on an Attic vase in Boston, showing two youths in the process of putting boots on their feet. We know they are dressing for a female chorus for one of them has already donned his mask, a young girl's face with the hair done up in a *sakkos* at the back; another identical mask lies on the ground between them. Although all these costume details and emblems can be incorporated into the figure of the god, it is also permissible to depict him with a minimum of insignia. Thus the chaplet of leaves and flowing hair with a wand of fennel is as characteristic as a pair of boots and a faun-skin. Flowing robes and a jug of wine, bare feet and a fillet only on the head would do just as well.

The other gods and demi-gods are not quite so loaded with insignia. Heracles, whose job it is to signify strength, wears only a lion skin and carries a bludgeon. In the *Frogs* of Aristophanes Dionysus appears in this disguise, much to the amusement of Heracles: " . . . Oh, 'tis enough to make a fellow hold his sides to see this lion's skin over a saffron robe! What does this mean? Buskins and a bludgeon? Where are you off to in this rig?" The whole of this passage must have been extremely funny to the Greeks and it gives us a revealing glimpse of what was considered masculine and what feminine.

Apollo's costume, again, varies considerably, but however he is dressed he always carries a golden bow and arrow. In Aeschylus' *Eumenides* Apollo himself threatens the furies with these weapons, " . . . quit my prophetic sanctuary, lest you feel the gleaming snake that darts winged from my golden bow . . ." Poseidon is always represented carrying a trident and Zeus usually has his winged shaft, signifying lightning.

The main point is that their emblems must in some way be significant of their characters, even if they are only something carried in the hand or worn on the head.

Jewellery

Jewellery is a particularly telling detail in the history of costume of almost any age, for it shows the wealth of a civilization and the artistic scope of the craftsmen in each century. It also helps – in any form of illustrative record – to define such characters intended to represent noble persons or moneyed classes and distinguishes their standard of taste in ornament. We can go deeper than this and make fascinating discoveries about the range of geological and geographical understanding of certain ages and marvel at the skilled craftsmanship exhibited in some fragmentary detail of personal ornament that has been made by an unknown workman in an age we consider uncivilized. It is in fact an endless source of interest and research.

Always in the past, particularly in ancient romantic writings, great store was set on those jewels and ornaments that came from vast distances, particularly the East. The Bible's descriptions of precious stones gives us to understand that they were mostly precious because they came from such distant lands. Each traveller or merchant not only suffered hardship on his daring expeditions but expected to spend years of his life in travel; therefore his prices were high. Such jewels were offered as gifts beyond price by kings and potentates, each travelling ambassador from another country came laden with the precious stones unfamiliar to the land where he expected to be received with kindness. We therefore find that such jewels decorate only the crowns and coronets, sceptres and persons of royal or religious leaders.

Most Greek jewellery was the work of skilled craftsmen who specialized in what we call goldsmiths' work. It was the sort of work that could be beaten by hand, pressed into a mould or cut from such stones as were available in the Mediterranean areas.

As we are interested primarily in the costume worn in the fifth century B.C. for the performance of the early tragedies and comedies it is sufficient for our purpose to know the type of ornament that would appear appropriate and possibly characteristic of some particular person, and not be an incongruous intrusion in an otherwise sympathetic costume design.

The hanging ornament is perhaps the most noticeable peculiarity of the

Fig. 28. Regal figures with golden diadems

age; this takes the form of beads or golden drops of simple bold design and they appear not only in the obvious capacity of earrings, but as the weights or tassels on the points of himations, their purpose to help the draperies to hang in the appropriate series of folds which is so very much a part of all Greek dress. Again, these same tassels or drops are attached to the girdles and many of the fillets worn around the head. They appear so frequently in design that they are at once a noticeable feature of the dress.

Brooches, pins and fibulae are the ornaments that secure the dress and these vary as much as any other item of ornament. Again they cannot be ignored because they are part of both the Doric and the Ionic chiton as well as being the only means of securing the himation.

Bracelets and rings appear in some considerable profusion amongst archaeological findings, but it would be useless to expect that a ring could have very much dramatic significance in the ancient theatre, though bracelets do appear on the arms of queens and great ladies.

Again, for identification purposes jewellery can be significant, though here we must face up to the fact that the majority of Greek jewellery was insignificant in size, apart from the very lovely diadems and crowns; it was its delicacy that made it remarkable.

Theatrically such crowns served a dual purpose: to distinguish regal characters and to support veils. Those illustrations that depict queens and princesses make a special point of using such crowns, and there is a passage in Euripides' *Hippolytus* where Phaedra asks her nurse to take off her headdress which " . . . weighs her brow . . .". Presumably they were as weighty as they appear in illustrations.

There are few dramatic references to other items of jewellery apart from pins and brooches. There is however the very telling description which is quoted elsewhere in this book about the necklace which Ion wore as a baby (see p. 13). There is certainly significance here and it is quite legitimate to assume that many items of jewellery took the form of charms and symbols.

Although each of these Greek ornaments in itself is a thing of beauty because of its fine craftsmanship, they are not particularly large or showy, certainly nothing in the nature of Byzantine or medieval ornament. Necklaces, for instance, were simple, sometimes only a small chain expressed by a line of dots on the drawings of the time. The tendency was to make them fairly close

Fig. 29. Varieties of crowns and hair arrangements

fitting, with any ornament there was splaying out from the main chain, something resembling leaves or petals linked together on one side only. The accompanying drawings show simple varieties of fifth-century goldsmiths' work. Crowns and diadems, on the other hand, were most impressive and dignified; the ornament on a queen's head would be at once obvious and regal. The motifs used in the design of all the jewellery stem from the familiar forms. Most of these have already been mentioned in the chapter on fabric design, but we do find the addition of fruits and foreign flowers such as the Assyrian lotus flowers and buds, pomegranates from Sparta, etc. Many of the pins were made from ivory, bone, amber or crystal and not necessarily bronze or precious metals. Certainly crystal appears in quite a number of personal ornaments though there does seem to be a distinct lack of evidence of the use of coloured stones (apart from amber, which is not a stone!). Earrings which were attached to the ear by a hook usually consisted of hanging drops of stones or golden ornaments some inch or more in length. Two particularly lovely examples with the wheel or flower form at the top appear illustrated below. The use of figures is not unusual and gods or goddesses are represented as often as animal forms. Snakes of gold or bronze are one of the most familiar designs for bracelets, a design so old in time that there seems to be no origin for it. All other bracelets appear to be narrow and nothing like the wide oriental bracelets. Delicacy and fragility are the main qualities to be observed, so that in dressing a play some care should be exercised in this respect. Normal theatre jewellery tends to be barbaric and over-emphasized because it is usually intended to express grandeur. The Greek illustrator never uses this particular form of expression.

The subject as a whole is a highly specialized one and many scholars and archaeologists have given us detailed descriptions of their findings.

Fig. 30. Golden earrings from Heracleum Museum, Crete

In any modern production the question inevitably arises as to what sort of jewellery can be worn. Each actress concerned would perhaps like to wear her string of pearls or some other gew-gaw. We must impose some sort of limit. I would suggest that we confine ourselves to the sort of ornament that could have been made from the materials that were available to the fifth-century craftsman.

For anyone with facilities to do so, a visit to the British Museum could be most rewarding, for here are necklaces and pins in variety. Otherwise, discretion must be exercised in the choice of any sort of ornament.

One other aspect of personal ornament which does concern us and cannot really be placed under the heading of jewellery is that of such things as fans, hand-mirrors and sunshades. All of these apparently modern conceits are to be found in the illustrations of the day, and they could be of use in certain scenes that do require such props. Their correct use is sometimes something of a

Fig. 31. Royal female figure with snake bracelets, crown, earrings, necklace and fan

problem. It is doubtful, for instance, if ladies habitually carried fans. We see pictures of seated queens with fans in their hands, or slaves using fans to cool their mistresses. They are even used as wall decorations. But to imitate the eighteenth-century flirting and fluttering of fans would be an anachronism. Hand-mirrors of polished silver or bronze were also used to identify the great lady. As far as sunshades are concerned, although their construction seems to be remarkably similar to a modern umbrella, they were not used or carried in the manner to which we are accustomed. They appear held over the heads, once more, of great persons, used, no doubt, as a movable awning which could be carried by a slave as a protection from the sun; not a thing to be toyed with or used as a walking-stick as those of our direct ancestors.

CHAPTER IV

Dramatic costume and footwear

Let us now direct our attention towards what little information there is available about the costumes which have in the past been considered by serious students of classic drama to be those worn by actors in the fifth century B.C. These clothes, that to our eyes have a splendid dramatic quality, seem to be used by artists of the time to indicate themes that do possibly bear on our knowledge of dramatic types, but it is futile to insist that this is a fact. We may assume that, in order to make the character outstanding, the artist has fully employed his knowledge of contemporary clothes that he has seen on some special occasion, such as a dramatic festival or perhaps a procession in the streets. Wherever it was, we now have records of these highly decorated garments and their use to us in the present day as a method of showing a majestic figure in Greek tragedy is of considerable value.

The vital difference between the normal civil attire described on the preceding pages and this dramatic costume lies in a very simple fact, that dramatic costume is based on a peplos or tunic and not a chiton.

Suppose we contemplate the chiton and its limitations. What do we find? A straight, free garment, restricted only at the waist, looking as if it were the easiest thing in the world to wear. The unfortunate fact soon presents itself, however, that this is an incredibly difficult garment to wear with any elegance. By this I mean that its very shapelessness tends to make it drop or sag into uneven and unsightly lines. Its fullness inevitably collects in certain places, making bundles of pleats just where you don't want them. The shoulders slip, the pins can drag, in fact it is the easiest thing in the world to disarrange. At the same time, it can look magnificent and eminently dignified when it is arranged with skill.

Now, if we are to believe the evidence of vase painting, it appears that there was a peplos type of garment which, instead of having pins on the shoulders, was joined on to a neckband or yoke which sat squarely on the shoulders and restricted the fullness of the garment itself. Any fullness was then held in place by a belt; not just a thin girdle but something wide, strong and decorated. This is the type of peplos that is referred to as "dramatic costume" by Pickard-Cambridge and other authorities. From an entirely practical point of view,

Fig. 32. Kings, princes or heroes

the theory is eminently sensible, for such a dress would be much easier to keep in order, there would be no restriction of movements, and no chance for the garment to get out of place. It is, in fact, far easier to move about in because it is made from a limited amount of material.

The garment appears to be roughly square in shape, folded and joined down the front and attached to a decorative yoke; sleeves are either attached just off the shoulder or else worn on some sort of undergarment. It is quite possible that the whole is woven in the form of a cross, as previously suggested, but we are not in a position to be sure of this. The shape emerges as a well-cut tunic, covered with richly varied and bold designs, with a neckline that fits and shoulders that are slightly shaped.

Clearly defined patterns of characteristic boldness appear on all such garments, not only deeply decorated borders and spot designs but patterns which tend to accentuate the waistline in the familiar cheating-the-eye manner so dear to Greek architects. Sleeves are variously decorated with chequered squares or diamonds, rings and running designs from shoulder to wrist. Each garment is as different and distinctive from its neighbour as pattern used with discretion and thought could devise. We do not know the colours that were used but there is little doubt of their distinctive quality and effect.

The sleeves are particularly interesting, again from a dramatic aspect, for although they vary considerably in pattern, they are always wrist-length. It would seem reasonable that a man playing a woman's part would be at a disadvantage should his arms be uncovered, for no man's arm can ever look like a woman's, especially at a period when muscular development in a man was considered a thing of beauty. If, however, the arms are covered, the face is masked and the robes reach the ground, it is very much more likely that the actor would carry off his female impersonation with both dignity and grace. A comparison arises today with school plays when boys are taking women's parts: however beautiful their voices and faces may be, there is probably only one boy in a thousand who could display his arms and hands bare without their incongruity being immediately noticeable. Probably for the same reason these "dramatic costumes" fitted the neck quite closely, for it is unusual for a man to have a neck as slim as that of a woman; they also came to the ankle in length, giving a maximum amount of freedom in movement with a minimum of noticeable physical form.

This, then, is the sort of garment that might have served a useful purpose for the tragic actor of the fifth century B.C. But it certainly does not rule out the possibility that other types of chiton and tunic were worn. It would seem most likely that such a garment was used for the main actors because it would make it easier for them to effect those lightning changes of costume which certainly had to be done somehow, and it could be relied upon to define immediately the character the actor was temporarily representing. We have to remember that, at this time, we are considering the problem as it applied to the two or three actors playing several parts. If, as we are given to understand, some of the actors made short appearances doubling for each other, it is reasonable to suppose that a complete disguise with definite characteristics such as

Fig. 33. Veiled female characters in dramatic costume and himations

masks and some very obvious colour or design on the costume itself, must have been used. Aristotle, writing in the middle of the fourth century, clearly informs us that only three actors took part in each of the contests, so that some such quick change was absolutely essential to the performance.

It is doubtful whether, in these days, many producers would care to limit themselves to a performance arranged on these lines, for, apart from the experimental value, such an exercise would cause unnecessary chaos backstage; but I hope that the above analysis makes the problem of the so-called dramatic costume a little easier to understand, and explains the position of importance that has been given to those illustrations that show these types of garments worn by figures who might be the leading actors in classic tragedy. When considering this aspect of costume we must also remember that a whole year went into the construction and rehearsal of a single performance. Every part of such a performance had to be considered with infinite care in order to bring out its full dramatic significance, for this was a competition. Every movement was judged, as far as we know, at a very high standard, and the smooth running and gymnastic ability of the main actors were all part and parcel of the exercise. To a civilization who cared so much for the arts and found so many uses for beautiful sculpture and decoration in their daily life, costume in dramatic production must have ranked quite highly in the hierarchy of visual arts. So much, then, for the garments that were probably worn by the actors. We may assume that they were a simplified version of civil attire with the maximum of arresting pattern.

Two very necessary details of dress still have to be given some careful consideration. However important the dress itself is, it is quite valueless as a significant disguise without the appropriate headdress and footwear. An actor's movements are governed by what he wears on his head and his feet. This is true of any period; perhaps the most obvious example of this occurs in Restoration comedy, when the actor finds himself compelled to walk about the stage in high heels and to restrict his head movements to accommodate a full-bottomed wig. In learning to cope with these encumbrances he is also learning how a gentleman of the seventeenth century came to terms with the extravagant foibles fashion compelled him to wear. Some of the mannered gestures of the Restoration must impose themselves naturally because of such restrictions; the necessity to keep the hair off the shoulders at certain times and to walk firmly on high heels. As soon as we consider these particulars in relation to classic theatre we come up against two very obvious snags. The first is that the classic actor wore a mask, and this mask appears to us to be a very exaggerated type

Fig. 34. Two costumes for Medea, both having the Asiatic headdress

of headdress with a contorted facial expression. The second is that a tradition has grown up which insisted that he also wore thick-soled boots raising him six or seven inches from the ground. It would be as well to consider both these problems separately, for they do need a great deal of sorting out. Their use or misuse has been such that there is still considerable confusion between tradition and origin.

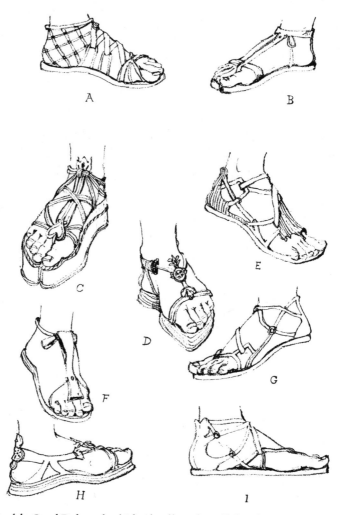

Fig. 35. Sandals. C and D show the thick sole of later date; all the other examples are taken from 5th & 4th century B.C.

First of all let us consider the boots. The Greeks were not, as far as we know, embarrassed by their footwear. Sandals were very light and free, tied or fastened with straps in a variety of ways over the foot and around the ankle. The soles were not thick. Their boots or buskins were also light and made all in one without a separate sole or with a very light sole that did not impede them in any way. Unfortunately the Romans saw fit to include the thick-soled shoe of their time into the traditional costume of the tragic actor.

It is curious how certain fashions of one particular decade can cling like leeches to some older traditional style, and eventually be passed down to the succeeding generations as unquestionably authentic. In our own era this has happened more than once. The beefeaters make a particularly interesting example of a case in point, for they are always accepted as wearing the costume of the time of Elizabeth I. In actual fact they do nothing of the kind; they wear eighteenth-century knee-breeches, stockings and buckled shoes, and a sort of early-Tudor-cum-nineteenth-century coat. The sole remaining items of Elizabethan clothing are the ruff and hat, and even the ruff has been cut down to a mere shadow of its original self. Nevertheless, many guide books to London inform visitors that this is the identical costume worn in the time of Elizabeth I.

The same sort of thing can be seen to have happened during the centuries in which Greek tragedy was being metamorphosed into "traditional Greek tragedy" by the Romans. We cannot say definitely that the high-soled boot is not to be associated with Roman staging, for there is some sort of evidence

Fig. 36. Roman tragic actor, 2nd cent. A.D.

to give substance to such a theory. There are, for instance, various small figures in terra-cotta as well as the famous ivory statuette from Rieti (now in Paris, see Fig. 36), which clearly show the actor standing upon what appear to be stilts of wood or cork which raise him some six or seven inches from the ground. We cannot be certain that such stilts or soles were not originally intended as pegs on the figures with which to fasten them into some sort of base. They are not as expertly shaped as one would have expected if they were intended to represent something wearable, like, for instance, the thick pantoffle type of shoe that was worn during the sixteenth and seventeenth centuries of our era. Further proof of something of the sort being worn is to be found from the mosaics from Porcareccia in the Vatican, but these are all of a much later date, probably late second century A.D., and possibly represent some form of traditional drama. The failure to distinguish between traditional and historic dress

Fig. 37. Two Roman ladies, 2nd cent. A.D. British Museum

has always been a barrier to a proper understanding of significant stage costume. The headdress of the Rieti figure is not so very different from the fantastic hairstyles worn by the fashionable woman of the second century A.D. (see Fig. 37). As a result of this we can see that complete blind spots occur even in the works of notable scholars and artists. Some of Charles Kean's productions in the nineteenth century illustrate this perfectly (although Charles Kean prided himself on archaeological exactitude he was, presumably, perfectly content to permit Mrs Kean to appear on the stage in the part of Lady Macbeth wearing a pink crinoline). However, the theory that was accepted for a great number of years that classic actors did wear thick-soled boots has, fortunately for all concerned, been recently disproved. Even if Roman tradition did encumber the tragic actor with *cothurnus* and a mask with exaggerated features and built-up headdress, *onkos*, neither of these is helpful to the actor's movements. It may have been practicable for some such exaggeration on the Roman stage, for we are given to understand by the best authorities that the Roman stage was merely a shallow high platform raised against a towering façade where dialogue and over-emphasized gesture took the place of acting. For this degenerate form of theatre some sort of caricature in the gesticulating eerie figure might have been necessary; indeed Roman figures and paintings of tragic actors show these exaggerated gestures. In the ancient theatre movement and spectacle played their part.

The boots worn by the Greeks vary in almost every drawing, but we

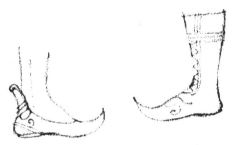

Fig. 38. Persian slippers and boots or buskins

are quite certain that the sole was light. In most instances where Dionysus appears his boots are a type of soft boot with a turned-up toe mentioned by Aristophanes as Persian buskins in several plays. One instance occurs in the *Clouds* – a bit of nonsense about dipping a flea's feet into wax: " . . . dipped its two feet in the wax which, when cooled, left them shod with true Persian buskins". If this is the buskin laughed at by Heracles in the *Frogs* and already established in classic theatre as a disguise for the male foot when appearing in the female chorus, we are perhaps a little nearer the true meaning of his jibe (see p. 56). Aristophanes also mentions Persian slippers as being essentially feminine in his *Ecclesiazusae*, for one of the husbands has his Laconian shoes stolen by his wife and finds it necessary to try to wear "those little Persian slippers" that she has left in their place. Aristophanes is far more articulate about fashions, if we can call them such, than any of the other great dramatists. His particular interest seems to be directed towards foreign fashions, and in much the same way that Chaucer picks out such strange things as a "Flanderish beaver hat" as a contemporary peculiarity and something worth comment, so Aristophanes mentions Persian slippers, Laconian shoes, Spartan shoes, Amorgis silk, Persian cloaks and so on.

Other boots are shown laced in the front, sometimes even with the toes quite free, the tops ornamented with the skin of some animal. This type of boot remained in use right through the following centuries until late Roman times, the only noticeable difference being that the sole gradually became thicker and the embossed design on the side developed into a fashionable extravagance, in Roman times gilded and perhaps jewelled. A perfectly straightforward calf-high riding boot also first makes its appearance on the horsemen depicted on the Parthenon frieze. This sort of boot does not lace but appears identical with the boots worn for riding throughout the middle ages and probably right up to the time of the introduction of the heel in the late Elizabethan period. On the accompanying pages I have done my best to illustrate the varieties of sandals that are shown worn by both men and women during this time. A Roman sandal as worn by the third-century figure of a young girl in the Delos Museum shows that, although the sole is indicated as an inch or more thick, it has been shaped so that there is an indentation between the big toe and the others (35C).

Quite apart from theories and proofs of the use of the cothurnus we do know that a thick-soled sandal was a very fashionable item in Hellenistic dress. This sandal, so different from the flimsy and elegant sandals of the Greeks, was probably made with many layers of leather. From the many sculptured examples of such a sandal it is obvious that this was a fashionable and elegant feature of dress and not, as we might expect, a sensible or serviceable one. It might even have been used as a form of class snobbery to indicate, in the same way as the Chinese foot-binding, that the wearer was in such luxurious circumstances that walking was not necessary.

This, then, is a rough statement that should help us to understand the limits of designs in footwear.

CHAPTER V

Masks

The fascinating study of masks has probably caused more headaches and misunderstandings than any other in the history of classic theatre. The chief difficulty is that there is very little evidence available concerning the masks worn for the early tragedies and comedies; yet there is a vast amount of information to be found during the late Hellenistic and Roman periods. This is a quite natural but infuriating state of affairs. We are interested primarily in the lifetime of the great dramatists, a comparatively short period of a hundred years – whereas the period that came after, which is still sometimes referred to as classic, lasted roughly six hundred years. There is, therefore, considerably more information to be had about the masks that were used by actors from the Hellenistic times (late fourth century B.C. onwards), and these were quite obviously stylized versions of the original. Examples of fifth-century masks clearly show us that they were not exaggerated but representational.

It appears that during the late fourth century there was a general tendency to create an exaggerated kind of mask, both for tragedy and comedy. This emphasized and enlarged the features in every way so that the mouth was made much bigger than life and always appeared wide open, expressive of agony or laughter as the case might be; the eyes were made larger or smaller than normal and the hair built up in the front of the head to form a crest or crown. In most instances the whole mask was much bigger than life. This form of hairdressing or building-up (*onkos*) is peculiar to the masks only from the fourth century onwards; by the beginning of the third century this particular feature had become an established and recognized feature of theatre costume.

The sources of our written information on the theatre come from the hands of Roman scholars. It is therefore not at all surprising to find that what was to them a traditional and well-established formula governing the playing of the old tragedies and comedies was accepted without further question as the original classic method of presentation. The Romans were hardly in a position to do any extensive research into the styles of four centuries earlier; it is only of comparatively recent years, when both travel to the ancient sites and photography have made research so much easier, that a grain of doubt was sown in the minds of scholars, especially when more extensive study of fragments of pottery disclosed the fact that during the fifth and fourth centuries B.C. such masks as were illustrated did not entirely conform to the descriptions given by Julius Pollux. This, then, is one of the misunderstandings which I hope is clarified. There is yet another which is almost as troublesome and arises from the primitive use of masks, that of disguise or identification. Tradition makes the classic mask an invention of Thespis who was supposed to have given the first performance of tragedy; in order to do so with realism he chose to disguise his face. In the first stages, we are told, this was done with a make-up of some sort, but gradually the idea of a mask to obliterate expression was carried into practice and a plain linen mask was invented. This story completely ignores or by-passes one of the primitive uses of masks – that of striking terror or awe into the hearts of any audience by the presentation of an inhuman and static head on a body that is human and moves. Masks have been used for this purpose since the beginning of human consciousness, and to this day they are still used expressly for this purpose by certain peoples. Witch-doctors and mystic dancers alike all over the world have found this sort of disguise or identification of supreme use to endow their movements with a sense of unearthliness. A mask can hold an audience spellbound, shocked or mesmerized; such qualities could not have been unknown to any actor at any time. Even the Corinthian helmet with its frightening face-piece was invented before Thespis.

Curiously enough the comic mask as it has come down to us is not a laughable thing unless one is prepared for it. However funny the expression may be, the same inhuman quality exists and any small child will be frightened by its first vision of anything so like and unlike reality. So the story of Thespis' mask would seem to be as out of date as many other theories that surround the theatre of ancient Greece. Perhaps it was a mask of linen that Thespis invented, something modelled and shaped into a firm structure that looked more lifelike than those of wood or other less plastic materials. It could not have been the first mask. The introduction of a tragic mask, coloured and modelled with impressive grandeur, is attributed to Aeschylus.

There remains no definite evidence as to the exact details of such masks, for naturally there is none in existence. The very fact that they originally had to be light enough in weight to be worn by any actor in reasonable comfort rules out any possibility of their survival. We are not aware of their actual construction, although various artists illustrated them from different angles and do show us some quite valuable and interesting points. We can see, for instance, that the hair was all part of the mask and not a separate wig. Such hair could have been human hair arranged in a suitable manner and set after the fashions of the day. It could, on the other hand, have been made from some animal hair or some such substance as tow. Certainly in the later masks of the Hellenistic and Roman theatre, the hair is so stylized that it has very little similarity to human hair. The coarseness and over-exaggeration of the features required some treatment that was much larger than life. The mask itself was made from carved wood, cork or leather, or perhaps it was stiffened linen, moulded on a marble face in much the same manner as a papier-mâché one can be today. This idea is one that appeals to me, because, if this were the case, it might account a little for the vast number of mask heads that still exist. However, it would only account for a very limited number of such heads, for the majority of them are either much too large or much too small to have been used for this purpose. It remains an interesting thought.

What colours were used to establish the identity of different types of persons we have no idea, for it is useless to attach any importance to Pollux's views on the original tragic masks. His writings tell us specifically of the character masks existing in his own day, not of the tragic masks that could be identified with the works of Aeschylus. Some of them could perhaps be acceptable as a guide to the more general types that appear in Euripides' and Aristophanes' plays. Anyway we do know that masks were worn from the time of Aeschylus' tragedies, their purpose being primarily to identify the actor to his audience when he was playing two or more parts and had to make speedy and obvious changes of character. They were also worn by the chorus to give unity and credibility to a group of young men who were taking the parts of the chorus, which might be representing a variety of types, both male and female, old and young, foreigners and sailors, and even animals and birds. From the pictures that have come down to us it would seem that a chorus, more often than not, wore identical masks. They were almost always intended to represent a community without any individuality. Obviously the best method of fulfilling

Fig. 39. Four of the female chorus represented in the Tarentum Fragments (p. 93)

their purpose was for them to wear identical masks, though there does not seem to be any proof that costumes needed to be identical. So here again is a perfectly good *raison d'être* for the importance of the mask. We must remember that the vast open-air theatres, with their seating capacities for 17,000 and 14,000, would really need a clearly defined head with a simple formality about it that could be easily distinguished in the distance. The variety of colouring and features that occur normally in any collection of individuals could be best overcome by the use of masks.

We may assume that the early masks used by Aeschylus were neither exaggerated in expression nor size. Their colouring might, however, have been in some way distinguishing; whiter skin tone for women perhaps in normal choruses, though we do know that in the *Suppliants* of Aeschylus there is a reference to these young women being dark-skinned. Probably the *Persians* were also. Each chorus must have had a sufficiently obvious type of mask to prevent them in any way from becoming involved with the main actors in the play.

According to the fifth-century illustrations, then, the masks were not larger than life. They fitted the head closely and left no room for padding, for they not only covered the face but carried the ornate hair styles or headdress peculiar to the part played by the actor at that particular time. Thus a woman would appear with her hair dressed in the latest fashion if she were meant to represent a woman of fashion, or with her hair shorn if she were a character in mourning (e.g. Electra), with a crown or coronet if she were a queen, possibly with a flowing veil to cover her neck and shoulders, or with other useful defining headdress. Masks of old men were made with bald heads or long untidy white hair, and the masks of young men had flowing locks, carefully arranged or rolled up in the manner of fighting warriors.

A dramatic gesture that could be made was that of changing a mask to represent the same character under different circumstances. A frightening instance of this occurs in the *Oedipus Rex* when after he has stabbed his eyes Oedipus appears before the horrified audience in another mask bearing the same features with blood streaming from the sightless sockets. The same occasion arises during the performance of Euripides' *Cyclops*.

There were, of course, other types of masks to represent unearthly beings. Of these we have little information, but a well-designed mask, as I have already mentioned, could give an awful sense of terror to any audience. Such was the reputation of the Furies as they appear in Aeschylus' *Eumenides* that boys died of fright and women miscarried. The *Bacchanals* of Euripides are also described as having a terrifying appearance. They were wearing snakes and vine-leaves in their hair, which they had let down in their ecstasy. Other unearthly beings would, of course, include Io with horns and the Okeanids in *Prometheus*; the latter were water nymphs and probably wore their hair flowing. The satyr masks followed a convention of their own. These are so many illustrations of these creatures that there is little doubt that the masks worn to distinguish them were endowed with the same peculiarities. The skull was enlarged in front so that the forehead projected over the eyes, the exact opposite to what was considered classic beauty. The hair receded to baldness on top, showing the full roundness of the skull. There was black hair at the back of the head and a curly black beard. The nose was short and wide and the nostrils distended; the eyes slightly slanting up at the sides and the eyebrows pointed in an expression of permanent surprise. The ears were animal and pressed forward with tufts of hair on the top. Sometimes tiny horns are indicated as on the head of Pan. The forehead has slightly pathetic lines etched on it which give the whole face a curious attraction in spite of its ugliness.

What is particularly interesting about such heads is that the hair follows the prevailing fashions of the day. It is sometimes done up at the back in the bound cup-handle shape, a style normally used by young women (see Fig. 40). This is particularly incongruous when the back of the neck is shown, as in the diagram, with fat and ageing creases. The drawing opposite is taken from the head of a centaur, but obviously his features are identical with those of the satyrs and the hair style here is again unusual and effective, drawn back to the nape of the neck where it is fastened by a fillet. It is interesting to note that such fifth-century drawings almost without exception show the hair uncut. So much was this habit adhered to that even satyrs and centaurs are depicted in this contemporary style.

Masks of the old comedy of Aristophanes must have included birds, frogs and wasps; such beings had been illustrated by the archaic painters and by the Egyptians several centuries earlier, and we are at liberty to use our own imagination in this particular. They need not have been realistic, though certainly they must have been recognizable. We know that the masks worn by the chorus in the *Clouds* represented women (with noses), for this is discussed in the play (see p. 106).

Apart from the characters already discussed, the use of masks in a modern production, if such a production is done in a normal indoor theatre, is hardly necessary. Make-up and wigs could serve the purpose admirably as long as complete re-enaction of the original is not attempted.

If, however, some vast open-air theatre is available, the use of masks is immediately a very great help towards adequate staging, and the loss of individual facial expressions behind a static mask will give a sense of impersonality which is of the greatest help to the audience's understanding. Particularly

Fig. 40. Satyr heads

is this helpful with the chorus, whose task is usually a heavy undertaking, for they are in the orchestra for considerable periods of time and the wandering eye or some facial peculiarity could be a distracting element when their main purpose is to produce a sense of rhythm into the whole production.

For serious students who wish to make a study of masks there are no better authorities than Pickard-Cambridge's *Dramatic Festivals in Athens* and Professor Webster's *Greek Theatre*, both of which have adequate photographs of existing mask representations.

Headdresses

Whether masks are used or not, we must consider the styles of hairdressing that will give the right effect in any one particular play; for this a knowledge of the original hairdressing is necessary. Nothing looks quite so out of place as a modern coiffure worn with ancient costume; it turns the costume into a form of fancy dress and completely destroys any illusion of period.

Hairdressing in classic times was quite a fascinating and, apparently, time-consuming occupation. Such highly styled coiffures lent themselves readily to the designing of wigs for the masks, and the difference between the male and female could be accentuated in this manner, for we are now aware that the male and female costume was fundamentally the same. Women's styles are not in the least difficult to imitate, even if the hair is short, for a *sakkos* or little cap can be used to cover the entire head with the exception of a small curled fringe and some kind of sideboard or bunch of curls on the cheeks. If the hair is long or even shoulder-length there is immense variety in the ways in which it can be suitably arranged. Modern lacquer would undoubtedly be of the greatest use in this case, but beer can set hair both well and stiffly if it is applied about ten minutes before setting so that the malt has time to get slightly tacky.

There was a similarity between men's and women's hair styles; both favoured the effect of hair on the cheeks, a small curly fringe or the front hair set in a profusion of bubble curls. Women did not wear their hair loose as often as the men. There are, of course, many portraits of flowing hair, and in the fifth and early sixth centuries long hair arranged in crimped locks appears on the heads of gods and goddesses alike, but generally speaking the sakkos holds the women's hair in place. This headdress varies considerably from a crude headscarf tied on with cords or fillets (see Fig. 41) to a finely decorated cap with an ornamental tassel at the back or a tuft like a handle at the top. A gold fillet or diadem is often worn as a sort of frontal crown holding both the sakkos and the front hair in place. If the hair is worn down, as is that of the caryatids on the Erechtheum (Acropolis, Athens, and also one in the British Museum), the back part is twisted or plaited; each of these famous figures has her hair in a slightly

Fig. 41. Varieties of sakkos. Centre left: hair style from one of the Caryatids at the Erechtheum, Athens

different style though this is rather difficult to see in the position in which they are. The one in the British Museum is, however, a wonderful example and well worth studying. The style of these caryatids is unfamiliar inasmuch as there are no other examples like them in any museums in Greece, but this does not mean that the style was not taken from a model with her hair dressed in a contemporary manner, familiar to Athenians of the fifth century. There are dozens of vase paintings which show the hair unconfined except for a little bag worn at the extreme end of the hair (see Fig. 42). The majority of these paint-

ings, however, show the hair done up in a knot at the back, with or without a sakkos. Young girls and children are often represented with pony-tail hair styles, the knot high on the back of the head so that the hair at the nape of the neck is drawn upwards showing endearing little curls at the back. The styles of hairdressing must necessarily have been influenced by the texture of the hair itself. Many really curly effects were, without doubt, the natural fuzzy curl that is still to be found amongst Mediterranean

Fig. 42. 5th cent. woman's hair style

people. The more formal styles have that curious bent wave which is obviously artificial and could have been procured quite effectively by plaiting and setting in clay, which was a very ancient method of waving the hair. During the fifth century the fashion was for the back hair to be raised to the level of the top of the head itself so that the sakkos normally made the skull appear egg-shaped rather than round. Later, towards the beginning of the fourth century, the hair was lifted even higher above the head, showing a curly cluster from the front (see Fig. 29).

Men's hair styles of the fifth century were far more decorative than the women's. Adhering to the age-old convention that a man's strength was in his hair no warrior would ever dream of cutting his off. There are, of course, the notable exceptions when mourning is indicated, such as the instance of Orestes cutting a single lock of his hair and laying it as a token of mourning on his father's grave. The long hair was done up in a variety of ways, and probably let down for feasts and other domestic occasions. A fillet or perfectly plain band served to keep the hair in place and the variety of styles that developed from the use of this are innumerable. The front hair was usually curled in some way, probably depending on the type of hair itself. Clusters of bubble curls very tightly set and oiled had a formality eminently suitable for the decoration of masks. This stiff formality is a distinctive feature of the times. Plaiting and pressing were also used, for we see many paintings with thin, wavy strands of hair which look remarkably similar to the effect obtained if wet hair is plaited till it dries. The fillet, though plain for ordinary purposes, could be a most intricate design for festive occasions. The wreaths of golden leaves decorated with precious stones are still to be seen in many museums, as are the diadem shapes which stand up in a half coronet above the brow. Kings and princes and other noble characters or high officials are normally portrayed with this sort of fillet or crown. Beards were also treated with considerable care, often being cut into two or three tiers of set curls, but normally tapering to a rounded point and not a spade shape. This formal arrangement of curls lent itself readily to the treatment of any hair, both in sculpture and design. In fifth-century literature, references to the long hair of the men are so common that we can be sure that those in Homer are not exaggerations. They are at least a verbal guide to the fashions that remained traditional for several hundred years. When Menelaus slays Euphorbus in the *Iliad*, Bk. XVII, Homer says: "He came down with a thud and his armour rang upon him. His hair had been as lovely as the Graces' locks – he used to bind the little curls with gold and silver twine." This binding of the little curls is obvious in all fifth-century sculpture if one cares to search for such details; it also explains, in some measure, the amazingly formal arrangements of the long hair.

Hats of felt and straw were in use. The straw ones differ hardly at all from the common large straw hat that appears to be quite ageless. With its large brim and close-fitting crown, its purpose, then as now, was to protect the head from the heat of the sun and shade the eyes when travelling or working in the fields. This hat was worn chiefly by the country-folk in summer, and women are often shown wearing it over the head covering which is, in reality, the himation pulled up over the head. The variety of design in felt hats is almost endless. There seems to have been considerable competition over who could alter the shape of his hat the most by cutting pieces out of the brim or rolling and turning it up in various ways. Hermes' hats are different in practically every picture

Fig. 43. Varieties of men's stylized hairdressing

of him; sometimes they are frisky and similar to what we now term Robin Hood, sometimes nearly flat like an inverted soup plate, sometimes like a pudding basin pulled well down over the eyes and ears. The nature of felt when pressed seems to produce a little point in the centre; this small tuft is visible in many of the vase paintings. All such hats were termed *petasos*. Another form of headgear was the Phrygian cap, tight-fitting well down over the back

Fig. 44. Varieties of petasos or felt hats

of the head, high off the forehead and with a curved peak on the top. This was worn by shepherds and possibly other outdoor workers during the winter. *Pylos* was the name for any hat without a brim. These were often worn by young men in such a manner that the curls around their faces were pushed forward and the top of the head covered by what was in fact a skull cap with a tuft on the top. The fashionable woman did not wear any sort of hat other than the sakkos; a fillet or crown was often the only ornament on her head, but in dramatic representation a veil appears very frequently. Are we to suppose that this was a necessary ornament to indicate a queenly figure? Or would it help to disguise the fact that this was a man in woman's dress? The structure of the male neck is much more solid than that of the female and could possibly appear grotesque with a realistic mask of a woman. These points in dramatic costume are interesting but it would seem they are impossible to prove, even though we have the reference to Aeschylus' "veiled and inarticulate actors" (*Frogs*, Aristophanes).

We have now examined in some detail the possible costumes, headdress and footwear in which the actors of the fifth century B.C. made their appearance; we have also seen that there does seem to be some coherent connexion between these costumes and the dramatic characters who wore them.

When the original orchestras are considered in their majestic natural settings, something of the full significance attached to the gesticulating figures some dozens of feet below the main body of the audience can be more easily understood and appreciated. At a later date the size of the orchestra diminished, the acting area became more restricted and the audience more intimate. The need for such emphasis as had existed was no longer imperative, nor were the plays of the later playwrights to be compared in grandeur with the original dramatists' work of the fifth century.

The gorgeous garments seem to vanish towards the beginning of the fourth century (though they are still to be seen decorating some of the vases from northern Italy), and like practically all forms of art and design a weaker and less dramatic style emerges. The obvious and more noticeable details that change are as follows: the waistline is raised, the mask exaggerated, the *onkos* appears as a necessary enlargement to the head, and if we are to accept the wall paintings

Fig. 45. Two travellers

found at Herculaneum as examples of late fourth- or early third-century drama we can see that the actor and his mask have already hardly anything in common with the actor and his mask of a century earlier – apart from the fact that he still wears an ankle-length gown and a mask.

It was probably at this period that traditional theatre costume began to become established, and it is from examples of paintings where actors are shown, such as those at Herculaneum and Pompeii, that Julius Pollux bases his work on classic drama.

He describes the character masks and the colours of clothing peculiar to certain types – no doubt with accuracy as far as the information that was available to him went in the second century A.D. He does not tell us of the garments of many colours and rich design, for his knowledge stems from later sources than the fifth century B.C.

One more fact emerges amidst a welter of inadequate information, and that is that the Greek armour undergoes great changes during the Alexandrian period and develops into the body-fitting long cuirass whose shape follows the muscular and physical contours of the wearer, giving him something of gross over-development or "noble" proportions as portrayed in all Roman sculpture.

Should it be thought more effective to produce a classic play in the Roman tradition these are the points of particular interest. The pattern had gone out of materials, they were no longer woven with intricate design but are dyed with the dyes already described (see p. 15), and possibly sometimes woven in wide stripes of almost rainbow hues. The waistline is high (and it was from such high-waisted gowns that the early nineteenth century took its classic revival interest). The sandals or boots are thick-soled, though not necessarily so thick that walking is impossible, and masks have exaggerated facial expressions with open mouths and fantastic hair styles. If such an experiment is made it would be as well to bear in mind the fact that when these costumes were worn they were displayed in front of a façade on a narrow stage and not in the great orchestras of the Lycurgian period.

Something of the intimacy of television had taken the place of spectacular production; intellectual vitality and colour had been sacrificed on the altar of crude display. Roman taste had little in common with Greek culture, for the Romans wanted horrific experiences, and rhetoric had taken the place of drama. Tragedy they had in abundance with their bestial sports, and the scholars who saw fit to write for posterity of a culture they could barely envisage were as uninformed as Stow was when he wrote his history of the middle ages at the beginning of the seventeenth century. Witchcraft and legend played as much part in Stow's history – fascinating as it is – as legend and hearsay did in the writings of Pollux and Vitruvius, two of our recognized authorities on classic drama.

CHAPTER VI

Chorus

It is especially the Greek chorus that presents almost insuperable difficulties to designers. Certainly there is a very real problem here, not easily overcome, for we are today completely unfamiliar with the feeling of dance and rhythm which originally served to assist dramatic performance. It was the chorus that set the pace, telling a story, creating tension, expressing depression or excitement as was required. Few deny the fact that such was the purpose of the chorus.

> Dancing expresses a feeling, and by expressing it, intensifies it; dancing in chorus (*la dance collective*), moreover, generalizes it: the same bodily movements repeated to the same rhythm by all the dancers inspire in them a common emotion and submit them to an emotional state which tends to impose itself even on the spectators. (Jean Rudhardt, *Notations fondamentales de la pensée religieuse et actes constituifs du culte dans la Grèce classique*, Geneva, 1958, p. 146.)

In primitive religious rites all over the world and at almost any period there is the same instinct for a chorus who, by their movement, chanting, or rhythmic monotony help to mesmerize an audience so that such sound and movement can control the pulse of the people, lifting them up, creating in them a variety of emotional experiences which might help the performance to greater dramatic heights. The Greeks of the fifth century were still near enough to the wild pagan rites that took place at the festivals of Dionysus to understand fully this form of sensuous attack. In Greek drama the chorus regulated the pulse of the audience who were in a sense hypnotized by its rhythm and cadences so that they were carried with the play and players into another world.

This is one of the many purposes of the chorus; how adequately this purpose was served is not for us to say at the present time, but it may help us to have a clearer picture of the essential unity of the dramatist's conception. This quality of rhythmic background cannot be expressed in costume unless the whole chorus be considered as a unit. In the same way primitive tribes disguise themselves by painting their faces, wearing skins or grass skirts when taking part in tribal festivities. Their function is to evoke a physiological response. Something of this is present in the Greek chorus although the purpose of the dramatist is primarily intellectual. This is an interesting theory for it is all of a pattern with the process of attacking the senses dramatically, to see, to hear, to feel swayed by the rhythm which is expressed in every way possible.

Thus it becomes impossible to ignore the chorus and the effect it must have made. Their costume is of great significance and it is not enough to borrow a dozen sheets and line the stage with a dozen superfluous characters draped in them. Each chorus must be governed by a oneness of some sort, be it texture, draperies or design. There must be a complete sympathy one with the other and total absence of obvious personalities. The masks were of the utmost importance and we can see in any illustrations where fragments of a chorus appear that they are always identical in any one play. By lack of personality I do not mean that a set of masks would do for any chorus in any play. Nothing could be more misleading, for in most of the plays the chorus represents a group of individuals such as elders, satyrs, Persians, young women or warriors. Each chorus must have the appropriate distinctive features.

Taking at random the names of some of the better-known plays, what do we find? *Suppliants, Persians, Eumenides, Women of Trachis, Bacchanals, Frogs, Birds, Clouds*; all these plays take their titles from the chorus. The chorus was therefore of great importance. Their place was the living foreground behind which the actors made their dramatic appearances; they were indispensable for this form of play. Aeschylus introduced distinctively dressed foreigners into both his *Suppliants* and *Persians*, beings from the underworld in his *Eumenides* and *Okeanids*, and the later playwrights with the exception of Sophocles followed his lead, making full use of contrasting types to add colour and form to their production.

Our limitations of actual stage area make the introduction of a chorus of this sort extremely difficult if not impossible, and only when a production can be performed in the round or out of doors can the full and proper use be made of a chorus. However, such experiments are undoubtedly interesting, and though the information about the ancient chorus is extremely limited the following facts and theories may be useful.

It is my intention to give any information that may be available to distinguish the various choruses from each other. To begin with, we do not know what the original costume worn by any chorus in the fifth century was actually like; there are so very few illustrations that give us the slightest idea of their unity or that do in any way tie up with the plays themselves. In fact, there are only three or four instances where the potter artist has definitely illustrated figures with masks who might be safely claimed to represent a chorus – we do not even know from which of the plays they may have been taken.

This leaves us fairly free to make our own selection from an assortment of suitable material. In each case the chorus must be considered as a moving pattern representing the types of persons referred to as chorus in each play. Their identity is always mentioned in the text and there are a few pictures which show similarly clad characters that correspond to the type of being that a certain chorus is intended to represent.

Let us consider two particularly interesting illustrations, both of which appear in Pickard-Cambridge's *Dramatic Festivals at Athens* (Figs. 28 and 41). Figure 41 I have redrawn, as the original is so fragmentary (p. 78). One of these is the famous volute-krater from Ruvo at Naples dated late fifth century. This shows a satyr chorus with their leader Silenus holding the mask of a bearded man with a coronet on his head. Silenus wears a form-fitting garment of wool or fur, like an old-fashioned pair of combinations, and over his shoulder is slung a leopard-skin (Fig. 46).

The satyrs are dressed in the accepted and traditional style peculiar to the species, a pair of fur trunks with a horse's tail behind and a leather phallus in front. A certain individuality is allowed in each instance. The fur, for instance, is represented in different textures: one satyr has his made from leopard-skin, another seems to be wearing leather trunks cut or ornamented on the side with a definite star flower pattern; but in each case the masks are identical and conform to the description already given on p. 80. The motif of a flower or ornamental disk at the sides of the trunks is not an isolated example of an artist's fancy; other pictured satyrs are shown with this peculiarity, so that we may reasonably assume that it was a familiar design used by actors when representing satyrs. In purely mythical pictures they do not wear any clothes at all.

The other collection of fragments, which is equally interesting and, according to Pickard-Cambridge, by the hand of the same painter, represents a female chorus. These fragments are from Tarentum, now in Würzburg (see Fig. 39).

Fig. 46. Satyr actors and Silenus from the volute-krater in Ruvo (Naples)

They again show clearly identical masks, very white with black curly hair cut short, probably denoting a tragic chorus in mourning. I have naturally been compelled to take a certain amount of licence in the redrawing of these figures because in their present fragmentary state there is only one figure that is anywhere near complete, but it is very doubtful if we had the whole of the original drawings that they would have furnished us with much more detailed information. Once the formula governing the design of these robes has been thoroughly digested there should be no difficulty whatever in composing suitable details to decorate such costumes in the same manner. It is particularly interesting to note that in this instance the chorus wears decorated peploi, as rich in design as those of many of the important leading actors. The theme of the play may have been one which needed some such striking chorus, but the fact remains that of even the very few fragments of figures with masks which we now possess, one is an example of a female chorus wearing dramatic costume. The costumes are particularly interesting for they are made in this manner already described as "dramatic costume" (see p. 64). They are not identical but they are similar. Bands of decoration appear in each case from neck to waist, the sleeves are long and tight-fitting, the main part of the garment has a small spot pattern embroidered or woven into it, and the hem has a deep border from ankle to mid-calf. As there are only a few of these figures that we can see, it is impossible to tell if one of them is intended to be the chorus-leader, but only one of them has a wide design at the waist, so that it is quite possible he is intended to be more important than the others. The effect of such a chorus would be one of a uniform pattern, especially in movement.

Both of these examples are tremendously interesting though we must be wary of accepting them as real illustrations from a play. They do give us a sense of theatre which is lacking in those illustrations that do not show masks.

Starting with Aeschylus and finishing with Aristophanes these various choruses cover a vast ground and in all probability each performance of the same play was dressed slightly differently. There is no reason to suppose that the original designs were adhered to without influence from other sources of inspiration at different times.

Of one fact we are happily quite certain, and this is that at the time Aeschylus wrote the *Suppliants* (*c.* 465 B.C.), he himself intended that they, the chorus, should be wearing a distinguishing costume, something remarkable and obviously different from the normal Greek dress. From a few words taken from the play we can see that he wished to make it clear that they were both dark-skinned and dressed in barbaric and foreign clothes. "The king cries, 'from what land is this company that I address, with its strange un-Greek styles and luxurious barbaric robes and diadems? For this is not the female dress of Argos, nor yet of the land of Greece.'" Now, according to legend, the Danaids were the fifty daughters of Danus, king of Libya, and Libya was a strange land of

Fig. 47. Iacchus and a slave girl with yoked tunic

coloured peoples to the Greeks of the fifth century. The clothes of Egypt and the upper Nile were both gorgeous and highly decorated, probably also exclusively of linen, and vastly different in style from those of the Greeks. We are at liberty to search all available material on vases and wall-paintings of the period to discover just how the Egyptians and Libyans are depicted at this particular period of classic art. The results are intriguing, for we immediately make the discovery that these countries were not restricted in any way to the draperies of the chiton or himation. Their clothes were quite distinctly made up and often had figure-fitting bodices and even flared skirts. Long sleeves were as often worn as short ones, and belts of considerable width appear on what looks very much like a corseted waist. The bold, colourful patterns that were used were those that we associate with textile printing rather than weaving. Generally such illustrations were done by Greeks, but there were, in fact, several Greek cities on the north African coast. The normal method of illustrating an Egyptian woman at this time was in a long, straight tunic with a wide band of design around the neck and another running from neck to hem, with a belt or girdle of some sort worn at the waist. Ankles are shown free and the flimsiest sandals are worn. The hair is long and is much heavier in bulk than that of the Greek woman. This style is to be seen whenever an Egyptian slave girl is introduced into a picture, but the Danaids were princesses so that their clothing must be something far richer than this. The most outstanding difference in the male costume is that Egyptians are nearly always shown with shorn heads or hair cut short just below the ear. This very simple fact makes them immediately strange to a civilization accustomed to the flowing locks of their menfolk. They are, of course, dark skinned. Danus himself says in the play: "The sailors too I marked, their dark limbs conspicuous in white robes." This might have meant, of course, that they were slave sailors and not Egyptians by birth, but the point is made quite clearly that their skins must have been stained to show up to perfection against the white bleached tunics of linen normally worn by the Egyptian of that time.

Egyptian design was as different as possible from the forms which are endlessly repeated in Greek ornament, and this fact alone could be the reason for the phrase "luxurious, barbaric robes". The motifs used in Egypt were those from the floral and animal world of a different climate from that of Greece; birds from the Nile valley figure in many patterns and designs, the papyrus

Fig. 48. Possible varieties of dress for chorus. From left to right: Egyptian, young Greek, naiad, Greek, Egyptian or Libyan, Greek princess, Egyptian

flower and lotus bud and blossom, the great ships that sailed the Nile, strange fishes and reeds, domestic animals such as cats and ducks all turn up over and over again.

Again, the chorus for the *Persians* should make a fascinating contrast to other choruses, for the Greeks were perfectly familiar with the Persian costume and probably dozens of artists used this difference of clothing purely for the sake of variety. Firstly, the Persians wore trousers, and in a land where these garments were unknown they were probably as provoking as a kilt would be to a Frenchman. Early fifth-century paintings show these trousers as loose and baggy, similar to the modern pyjama trousers, with gay spot patterns or stripes. Later illustrations make them skin-tight like ballet tights, finishing at the ankle and showing a bare foot or else having a short boot. The patterns are the predominant features in them; stripes and rings, spots and checks appear in dozens of different arrangements. A particularly wonderful vase in the Naples museum shows figures in some considerable detail and variety. The subject illustrates Persians bringing their taxes to Darius with the gods placed above and an heroic scene running round the neck of the vase. Each of the figures is some five or six inches in height, so that there is ample space for details of decoration of their clothing. It was painted somewhere around 340 B.C., but still faithfully reproduces the styles of Persian clothes indicated a century or more earlier. Persians fighting Greeks appear on vases as early as 570 B.C. We are therefore aware of their styles of clothes before Aeschylus wrote the *Persians*. Over their gaily coloured trousers they wore a short, patterned tunic with short sleeves to just above the elbow, and long sleeves from some under-garment, probably like a jersey, show beneath the shorter sleeves. If a cuirass was worn over the tunic it was very similar to the Greek breastplate with the familiar hanging leather straps or apron from the waist. Frequently they wore a leather helmet with a peak on top, vaguely Phrygian in shape but with long hanging pieces at the sides which apparently could be fastened under the chin like a child's bonnet; a flap covered the back of the neck and shoulders and sometimes there was yet another pair of hanging flaps over the ears. Their swords were short and wide, occasionally rather like a scimitar in design, always wider than the Greek sword, and this is a point of interest. They were apparently bowmen rather than spearsmen; Aeschylus especially mentions this. A very free painting on a little vase of the fifth century in the British Museum looks exactly like the figure of

Fig. 49. Persians taken from the Persian vase, Museo Archeologico Nazionale di Napoli, 4th cent. B.C.

Punchinello from a Commedia dell' Arte drawing of the seventeenth century. These loose trousers do not seem to appear again after the middle of the fifth century. It would seem that the art of making tights had become established and the skin-tight leggings worn by all the Asiatic races look much the same in construction if not in design.

Such tricky beings as the furies in Aeschylus' *Eumenides* differ as much as devils or angels do under the hands of the various artists who illustrated our own religious drama. The same problems arise in each case: are we to understand that these illustrations are taken from dramatic performances or that they are the creatures of the artists' imaginations? This is a problem that must remain unsolved. Sometimes the furies are shown with wings and obviously illustrate the myth rather than the *Eumenides*. Sometimes they are quite ordinary figures with snakes coiled in their hair in the manner associated with the maenades, and they wear a short peplos, patterned or plain, and boots. Aeschylus, however, pictures them in a very different manner. There is nothing human in his first description. They are horrific and frightening in a particularly repulsive manner. In the first scene the Pythian priestess is terrified when she sees them asleep and snoring around Orestes:

> . . . a strange company . . . not women; gorgons – yet, again they are not like gorgons. Harpies I saw painted once, monsters robbing king Phineus of his feast; but these are wingless, black, utterly loathsome; . . . from their eyes distils a filthy rheum; their garb is wickedness to wear in sight of god's statues or in human homes. They are creatures of no race I ever saw; no land could breed them and not bear the curse of God and man.

There is vast scope here for any designer and only by the use of masks could such horror become convincing. Towards the end of the play it seems that the furies must change their costumes or don a cloak, for Athene says, ". . . young women, children, a resplendent company, flower of the land of Theseus, with a reverend troop of elder women dressed in robes of purple dye shall go with you".

The great majority of the choruses are citizens. With such a chorus the normal civil attire of the time probably gives the best effect. In the case of elders their clothing should show dignity and a certain uniformity. In no circumstances should the chitons be skimpy, for a sense of age can be much better expressed by folds of material than by anything figure-fitting. Nor should they ever appear comic. The adept use of an himation can also help the illusion of age. Here again we find the familiar problem of disguise: how to make young men appear elderly and frail. In all probability the use of sleeves and ankle-length chitons is the best answer; certainly ankle-length robes would endow such a chorus with the best possible means of introducing unity into their movements, and a sense of rhythm into every isolated gesture. A series of different length garments makes an unfortunate pattern, visually inharmonious. As our main interest in such a chorus is to help the play to an added sense of lyric style, it is important to introduce no discordant note in the appearance of the chorus and no identifiable details of personality. This is a general line that can be accepted and used with the majority of citizen choruses: trailing garments are to be avoided at all costs and too much leg is equally inadvisable. This may, perhaps, have been the reason why choruses in the original plays wore boots. Their legs, when they showed, would give a similar outline and not an individual one. There seems to be no instance when the female chorus was wrapped in veils. This was probably a wise principle to follow because of the difficulty of fixing a veil that does not shift or get out of place in movement. Also, as presumably all choruses were masked, a veil except as an extra small ornament would be quite unnecessary.

We have no indication of the sort of clothes worn by the sailor chorus in Sophocles' *Ajax* and *Philoctetes*. Something practical, plain and simple would seem the most sensible method of dressing them. They might wear a pylos on their heads or the leather helmet commonly worn by archers. Their tunics would be short and belted, but there is no sort of distinguishing uniform. All Sophocles' other choruses are citizens or slaves. There should be plenty of material that can be taken from the illustrations on these pages to give all the help necessary for the dressing of such characters.

Perhaps it is as well to mention here that slaves were not necessarily clad in rags and tatters. They were quite often honoured personages in a household whose master had bought them or brought them back as trophies of war because he was attracted by them and actually wanted them to become part of his household. The lower type of slave was probably of a lower mentality and therefore more useful in some menial capacity. Class distinction must have existed amongst slaves just as much as it does among other reaches of society.

When we get to the works of Euripides we find considerable variety in the type of characters he introduces into his choruses. There is a limited amount of written information about some of these choruses for, though the playwright gives us no stage directions, his descriptions from the mouths of his actors are quite vivid enough to be helpful. Particularly is this so with the *Bacchanals*, and in this weird and terrifying play we need all the help possible, for the theme is both savage and discordant and the chorus must create a sense of horror, just as

Fig. 50. Three slave characters in Asiatic or foreign clothes

much if not more so than the chorus of furies in Aeschylus' *Eumenides*. We are confronted with a band of women who are Dionysus' followers as well as the women and wives of Thebes. In the first few lines we learn that the main band of followers came from Asia and could well wear Asiatic costume. There is no indication that they have Amazons with them though the original legend insists that this is so. The whole chorus, then, is different, composed of old and young as well as foreign women. There is only one obvious visual connexion between them; whatever their dress, it is to be covered with a faun-skin, snakes as well as ivy or smilax must appear in their flowing hair and they all carry thyrsus in their hands. All this is clearly stated in several different passages.

There are also a number of illustrations depicting the Bacchanals or maenades joining in the ecstatic chase with Dionysus. A sense of violence and savagery must exist, for no formal chorus would in this case be the slightest use to the play. The following translation gives the instructions for the ecstatic dress: "Thebes, nurse of Semele, garland yourself with ivy; deck yourself abundantly with green lovely-fruited smilax, and consecrate yourselves with sprigs of oak or fir and deck your cloaks of dappled faun-skin with white curls of braided wool. And be reverent in your handling of the violent wands" (l. 105 ff.). Again (l. 695) the messenger describes the women working on the hill-side and how the madness affected them: "... and first they let down their hair about their shoulders and hoisted up their garments if the fastening was undone, and girded their dappled faun-skins with snakes which licked their cheeks ..."

Fig. 51. Bacchanal with thyrsus

In many of the pictures of the ecstatic dance, the maenades or Bacchanals are wearing the very full and pleated Ionic chiton. This sort of dress if it could be arranged successfully would without doubt add to the sense of disorder. The very fact of hitching up their garments would produce the uneven hemlines which do quite naturally give an effect of abandon and almost drunken carelessness.

The Phoenician women would probably have been represented in some form of oriental costume, possibly similar to the Asiatic style that Medea (p. 69) usually wears. On the other hand they could equally well wear the Egyptian type of dress worn by the Danaids (see Fig. 48).

Aristophanes is the only one of the dramatists who introduces animals and clouds into his choruses. Some of these unexpected beings might conceivably have had their inspiration from examples of archaic ornament or even from the animal-headed pictures of gods and goddesses of ancient Egypt. Whatever their origin we must look for our inspiration in design to those pictures that might

Fig. 52. Dionysus and Bacchanals with faun skins and snakes

have been available in Aristophanes' lifetime. The *Wasps*, we are told, really are dressed as wasps: "Look well at us and you will see that we have all the character and habits of a wasp." They wear wasp waists and stings, so no doubt their masks were equally appropriate, but we are also given to understand that they wear cloaks, for when preparing to do battle they cry, "Come, children, cast your cloaks to the wind, run, shout, . . ."

We are, however, not so clear about the visual reality of the chorus in the *Clouds*. For in this instance they are not so obviously disguised, nor are they meant to be, for the character of Socrates insists that clouds can take any shape, indeed look like centaurs in the sky; Strepsiades is equally insistent that they, the chorus, look just like mortal women to him and that he personally never saw a cloud with a nose. There is also some play about them looking like a sheepskin stretched out, but whatever sort of design is used for this particular chorus it must not completely obscure the fact that they give the appearance of women.

This is, in all probability, the only instance where the chorus is not wearing something which suggests the type of being they are supposed to represent.

In the *Birds* each member of the chorus is intended to represent a different type of bird. In the *Knights* we are not given the slightest indication of how they are supposed to look, but there is in existence an Attic vase with an interesting design showing warriors in armour sitting on the backs of other men who are wearing horses' heads (this is beautifully reproduced in Professor Martin Robertson's Skira book on Greek paintings).

From this very brief summary one definite fact emerges and that is that the chorus in each case appears in strong contrast to the main characters of the play. Such are the scattered facts that emerge from the plays themselves and only by coupling these with the contemporary illustrations shall we arrive at the sort of costumes we are seeking.

Index